BATTLES AND BATTLEFI
OF SUSSEX

A MILITARY HISTORY OF SUSSEX FROM THE IRON AGE
TO THE SECOND WORLD WAR

HISTORIC MILITARY PRESS

John Grehan

To find out about other titles produced by
Historic Military Press visit our website at
www.historicmilitarypress.com.
Alternatively please write to us free of charge at
Customer Services, Historic Military Press, Freepost SEA 11014, Pulborough, West Sussex, RH20 4BR,
or telephone our freephone number: 0800 071 7419.

HISTORIC MILITARY PRESS

BATTLES AND BATTLEFIELDS OF SUSSEX

A MILITARY HISTORY OF SUSSEX FROM THE IRON AGE TO THE SECOND WORLD WAR

© Copyright John Grehan, 2001.

First published 2001 by Historic Military Press,
Green Arbor, Rectory Road, Storrington, West Sussex, RH20 4EF.

ISBN 1-901313-12-3

Printed in the United Kingdom by
Selsey Press Ltd., 84 High Street, Selsey, Chichester, PO20 0QH
Telephone: 01243 605234

HISTORIC MILITARY PRESS
Green Arbor, Rectory Road, Storrington, West Sussex, RH20 4EF.
Telephone/Fax: 01903 741941

Cover: Arundel Castle from the air, (reproduced by kind permission of His Grace, The Duke of Norfolk).

www.historicmilitarypress.com.

CONTENTS

THE AUTHOR

John Grehan has written or contributed to more than thirty military history books, magazines and journals. His publications include books on the Peninsular War and the campaigns of the Duke of Wellington. John is a respected military historian whose work has received favourable reviews in both specialist journals and the national media. At the time of going to press, one of John Grehan's previous books, *"The Lines of Torress Vedras"*, had been short-listed for the Templar Medal Book Prize for British Military History. John lives and works in Sussex.

Praise for one of John Grehan's previous books "The Lines of Torres Vedras"

"a well written, closely argued and fascinating contribution to the historiography of the Peninsular War." - *Andrew Roberts, The Spectator February 2001*

"written with skilful economy ... essential reading". *Ray Cusick, Age of Napoleon Magazine*

"thought provoking" - *Minature Wargames August 2001.*

"written by a respected authority ... this is highly recommended" - *Military Illustrated Jan 2001*

ACKNOWLEDGEMENTS
I am grateful to Katherine Leadly of Cassell and Co., for permitting me to quote from Tim Newark's book, Celtic Warriors. Penquin Books allowed me to quote from C. Lee's This Sceptred Isle, Mercia Publications granted me permission to quote from D. Carpenter's The Battles of Lewes and Evesham, and Dilip Sarkar gave permission to quote from his book Bader's Tangmere Spitfires.

My thanks also go to Ray Cusick who edited and amended the penultimate draught of the manuscript and to my wife Lynne for the countless hours she spent by my side walking around the forts, castles and battlefields of Sussex.

For assistance with the illustrations I would like to thank His Grace The Duke of Norfolk and Mrs Sara Rodger (Assistant Librarian at Arundel Castle); Mr. D.F. Mace; Marcus Grehan and Leanne Swannie; Mr. Jeremy Knight (Curator, Horsham Museum); Mr. J. Manley (Chief Executive of the Sussex Archaelogical Society); Councillor Daley (Lewes Town Council); Mrs Mary Taylor; Mr. G. Bailey (Administrator, Bodiam Castle); Mrs C. Sterne (English Heritage Photographic Library); and Mr. I. Everest (Manager Newhaven Fort).

Introduction
The Military Geography of Sussex

From its south-eastern tip Sussex is little more than sixty miles from continental Europe and the county's coastline, some seventy-six miles long, occupies a large part of Britain's southern frontier. Before the days of Macadam and the Turnpike, water travel could prove more certain than land transportation and the seas that define the borders of our nation aided, rather than deterred, the invader. Though the last successful invasion of Britain took place almost 1,000 years ago, the gently shelving beaches of Sussex have tempted the prospective invader with the promise of both an easy disembarkation and a short and direct route to London.

The repeated threat of invasion from the Continent has shaped the very landscape of the county. The rounded tops of the Iron Age hill forts, the sheer walls of the medieval castles, the squat stumps of Martello towers, the moulded Vaubanesque contours of the Palmerstone redoubts and the crouched concrete blocks of the WWII pillboxes constitute the visible evidence of Sussex's position on Britain's front line.

Over the centuries, the coastline has changed. Selsey was once an island - its Old English name was *Seolesig*, or Seal Island. Pevensey castle, now around a mile from the coast, once stood on a small peninsula that projected into the sea. To the east of Pevensey, the town of Old Winchelsea was swept away by mighty storms and an entirely new town had to be built away from its once magnificent harbour, the Camber. Storms, shingle and silt also blocked Hastings harbour and coastal erosion took away part of the cliff where its castle once towered above the sea. The estuaries of the rivers Arun and Adur have shifted a number of times, driven by westerly winds and strong currents. The mouth of the River Ouse was once at Seaford. It is now at Newhaven.

Inland from the coast lies Sussex's most prominent geographical feature. Running for seventy-two miles from its origins deep in the heart of Hampshire to its conclusion, at the cliffs of Beachy Head high above the Pevensey Levels, is the chalk mass of the South Downs. Eight hundred and eighty-eight feet tall at its highest point and between five and seven miles wide, this natural defensive barrier was, like the sea, as much an aid to communication as an obstacle. To the north of the Downs is a narrow strip of greensand and then the Weald, once a vast, virtually impenetrable forest jungle which was almost devoid of lateral pathways. Only along the foot of the Downs, or across their lofty peaks high above the Wealden plain, could Neolithic and Iron Age man travel easily from east to west across Sussex and it was upon the broad peaks of these hills that the early inhabitants of this area built the first defensive fortifications. At Mount Caburn, The Trundle, Cissbury and half a dozen other sites the remains of the earthen ramparts and deep ditches of the hill forts can still be traced.

The Downs are dissected by three large rivers - the Arun, Adur and Ouse. These waterways were all navigable for a considerable distance inland from the sea and to guard the passage of these important commercial and strategic avenues great castles were constructed on dominating heights at the points where the rivers cut through the Downs. At a later date, when the paths of these rivers had settled, their estuaries were also guarded by solid Victorian forts. Some of these defensive works have been all but destroyed yet at Arundel, Shoreham, Lewes and Newhaven the walls of once-mighty fortifications still stand proudly in their historic settings. A fourth river - the Cuckmere - also passes through the Downs but the river is not navigable and is so close to the eastern limit of the Downs that it possesses little strategic value and no fortifications protect its upper reaches. However, the wide, flat estuary of the Cuckmere, known as Cuckmere Haven, was considered to be a likely disembarkation point and pillboxes and machine-gun posts dating from World War II now blend into the nearby cliffs.

Further to the east, close to the Sussex border with Kent, is the River Rother. As with all of Sussex's major rivers it flows from north to the south, exiting into the sea. At its estuary Winchelsea developed into one of the county's most important ports until the storms and the drift of shingle diverted the mouth of the Rother eastwards to where the town of Rye now stands. Throughout the middle ages and until the sixteenth century, Rye was considered to be one of the bulwarks of the nation. The prevailing winds in the Channel are from the west and the silt and shingle closed in upon Rye harbour, narrowing its passage and reducing its scour until the port was left far from the sea.

The Rother, with its tributaries the Brede and the Tillingham, marks not only the eastern extremity of the county, but also the limit of the most extensive region of flat land along the south-east coast - the Romney Marsh. The Rother, as the only defensible feature in the area, was of considerable military significance and its course was commanded by the most sublime of Sussex's fortified buildings, Bodiam Castle. The line of the Rother was also incorporated into the most ambitious military structure of the nineteenth century, the Royal Military Canal. The Canal, really a massive wet ditch and rampart, effectively isolated Romney Marsh and removed it from the military equation.

Confusingly, there is another River Rother in Sussex. This second Rother is in West Sussex. It is a tributary of the River Arun, which it joins near Pulborough. A station was built by the Romans at the junction of these rivers on Stane Street, the great road from Chichester to London. A Norman motte and bailey castle was also built near here.

Another river, the Lavant, has its origins in the western Downs, running southwards to meet the sea at Chichester. In early times the Lavant estuary, sheltered by Selsey to the east and Thorney Island to the west, was the most important waterway along the Sussex coast. It was here that the Romans built their regional capital, the fortified stronghold of Chichester.

At the eastern end of the Downs the hills fall away to the flat, low terrain around Pevensey and Eastbourne which travels on beyond the borders of Sussex and across the Romney Marsh. This is an area that is difficult to defend and every actual or potential invader from William of Normandy to Adolf of Germany has regarded the beaches of East Sussex and Kent as the best available landing ground. Here can be seen the powerful Roman fort at Pevensey which was one of the Saxon Shore forts built to deter the barbarian raiders. The castles of Hastings, Camber and Rye, and the seemingly endless chain of Martello Towers, still look out from this shoreline.

Paradoxically, the low-lying nature of the ground in this area lent itself to defence. The drainage ditches here are sealed by sluice gates and if invasion threatened the area could be flooded by opening the gates. Though this was official policy in the 18th century and early 19th century, it was never put into practice.

Northwards beyond the beaches and the Downs is the clay soil of the Low Weald which, in wet weather, turns into a heavy, glutinous mud. A travelling barrister in 1690 described Sussex as "a sink" which receives all the water from two long ranges of hills on both sides of it - i.e. the North and South Downs. A hundred years later, in 1751, a Dr John Burton in an account of his journey through Sussex asked : *Why is it that the oxen, the swine, the women and all other animals are so long-legged in Sussex? May it be from the difficulty of pulling the feet out of so much mud by the strength of the ankle, that the muscles get stretched as it were and the bones lengthened?*

The extreme north and north-eastern corner of the county, bordering Kent and part of Surrey, is occupied by the High Weald. This is a broad belt of sweeping sandstone hills and narrow valleys of clay or shale. Campaigning across such terrain would have been extremely difficult especially as the Weald was also partly covered in a dense forest (the word Weald means wood) which in Saxon times was recorded as being 112 miles from east to west and thirty miles across. The mud and the trees alone were a sufficient deterrent to any invaders from the north and few fortifications are found in the north of the county.

Despite its former inaccessibility this area has contributed significantly to the military history of Sussex. It was upon the Wealden hills to the north of Hastings that Harold and William fought for the crown of England, and the flat lands of the Low Weald played a part in the greatest conflict of all - World War II. At Hammerwood near East Grinstead and on the flat fields of Chailey, small, temporary airfields were formed and used from 1943 until after D-Day.

Like the Sussex coast, the Sussex Weald has changed considerably. Most of the great forest has gone, devoured by the iron workers and ship builders of previous centuries and the property developers of more recent times. The great medieval hunting grounds of the Ashdown Forest have been preserved, however, and these rolling heathlands have been a training ground for the British Army since World War I.

The other low-lying region in Sussex is the strip of land between the Downs and the sea. This coastal plain widens from the east until it reaches its broadest point at Chichester where it stretches for ten miles towards Selsey across what is known as the Manhood Peninsula. Here, during World War I, were seaplane and airship bases to protect allied shipping crossing the Channel and a generation later this coastline, so close to Nazi-occupied Europe, was the home of six airfields including Tangmere - the second most important fighter base in the south during the desperate months of the Battle of Britain.

At the western end of the Sussex coastline the featureless and almost rectangular shaped projection of Thorney Island also proved to be an ideal base for the RAF. The airfield was used by Coastal Command and then Fighter Command from 1938 until 1976 and Thorney Island is still occupied by the Army. Ford airfield was formerly the Fleet Air Arm's H.M.S. *Peregrine*, and Shoreham airport was once the home of Hurricanes and Blenheims.

A 1932 aerial photograph of the Littlehampton West Bank Fort which guarded the estuary of the River Arun, (By kind permission of Mrs. M. Taylor).

The South Downs - defensive barrier or Iron Age super-highway? This is a view from the Norman motte and bailey castle at Fulking looking towards the hill fort at Devil's Dyke.

1
Celts and Centurion
The first invasions of Sussex

There are few records to tell us of the conflicts that may have occurred in the Sussex area before the Battle of Hastings in 1066. The large number of fortifications that were built on the Downs, the High Weald and along the coast, however, clearly indicate that the threat to the local population of armed assault was indeed a real one.

The first defensive works that can be found in this area date back as far as the New Stone Age. These are the "causewayed" enclosures of Neolithic man. There are at least four such New Stone Age camps in Sussex, at The Trundle (north of Chichester), Barkdale (above Bignor), Whitehawk (Brighton racecourse) and Coombe Hill. They were sited on the Downland summits and they were formed with earthen ramparts above one or more ditches. The entrances were approached along causeways which bridged the ditches and cut through the ramparts to reach the interior.

These camps were also used as corrals for rounding up cattle. Populations were small in Neolithic times and it is likely that conflicts between tribes were not common. It is therefore possible that ranching was the main reason for the existence of the enclosures, as with the Bronze Age camps such as Ranscombe near Lewes, defence being of only secondary importance. [1]

There can be no doubt, however, about the primary purpose of the Celtic forts of the Iron Age. The remains that we see today at places such as Hollingbury, Wolstonbury and Highdown were made by the Celts who arrived in the Sussex area around 550 BC towards the close of the Bronze Age in Britain. These forts were of a similar construction to the causewayed enclosures, with deep ditches hewn out of the chalk and high ramparts made from the excavated earth, topped with wooden palisades. The earthen walls were revetted with timber and in at least one fort - that at Hollingbury - the revetments were reinforced with flint walls.

Other Iron Age forts have also been identified in the Weald - notably the promontory forts at High Rocks and Iping and the hill fort at Garden Hill in Ashdown Forest- which does indicate that this area was not the uninhabited wilderness that it was once believed to be. [2]

To defend such a fort, the defenders would hurl stones, and possibly javelins, from the ramparts. Pits filled with suitably-sized stones, the equivalent of magazines in fortresses of more recent times, have been found at excavated sites. [3] The weakest points in the defences of a hill fort were the entrances and it was against these that attackers concentrated their efforts. As Julius Caesar in the first century BC has explained, the attackers would attempt to drive the defenders away from the entrance with a hail of stones. Then, under the cover of their shields, they would try and set fire to the gate. Gateways, therefore, became increasingly sophisticated. Often the actual gate was set well back from the edge of the ditch with the walls flanking the entrance and gateway. It is even possible that elaborate gate-towers were built above the entrance to enable the defenders to throw stones onto the heads of the approaching enemy. At The Trundle, for instance, excavations have revealed that the gates had inverted entrance passages and that, when the last improvements were made to the fort around 200 BC, the gates were made even stronger and the passages longer.

Though some hill forts were permanently occupied fortified villages, most were likely to have been administrative or trading centres during times of peace. There is no evidence to suggest that they were the strongholds of local chieftains but more probably places of refuge for the community if threatened by an aggressor. Gradually, the smaller hill forts fell into disuse with the larger ones becoming tribal headquarters.

Around 250 BC a second group of Celtic warriors crossed the

Channel. They came from the Marne area of France and were armed with a new and formidable weapon - the horse-drawn chariot. [4] In the face of this invasion the local Celts built more hill forts and strengthened the existing ones but the Marnians could not be deterred. The invaders successfully occupied the western and central Downlands establishing their capital at Cissbury (near Worthing) where they built the second largest Iron Age fort in Britain. The walls of this impressive structure are a mile in circumference and encompass an area of seventy-eight acres. The surrounding ditch was originally eleven feet deep with ramparts thirty feet wide, towering twenty to thirty feet above the ditch. It took approximately 60,000 tons of earth and stone, reinforced by between 8,000 to 12,000 timbers, to form the walls. [5] It would have taken a huge number of warriors to man these defences adequately.

Cissbury was also England's second most productive flint mining site. Flint was Neolithic Man's axe-head, arrow-head, spear tip and dagger. Cissbury was a great regional arsenal where weapons were made and stored and the site must have been as important in the Stone Age as it was in the Iron Age.

The Celts were the dominant nation of the pre-Roman era throughout Europe. They were a mixture of racial types linked by a common language and their settlements extended from Asia Minor to the Atlantic. Celtic society was not as uncivilised or barbaric as the Romans, who supplanted them, have led us to believe. In general the Celtic leaders were elected to office and it was their duty to administer to the community. When a tribal group occupied a territory the land it held belonged to the tribe as a community and the ground was shared out by the drawing of lots. Their religion was Druidism which was one of the first religions to preach the doctrine of the immortality of the soul. Many Romans considered that it was this belief in immortality that led to the Celts reckless bravery in battle. Indeed, the Druids would accompany them into battle.

The Celts were excellent iron-workers, able to produce weapons that were lighter, stronger and sharper than the bronze weapons of the people in the regions they overran. Their leaders fought on horseback armed with throwing spears (or javelins)

and long iron swords. They were considered to be the finest light cavalry in Europe using their javelins in hit and run raids against enemy infantry formations. The lower orders operated on foot. They used both thrusting spears, which could be up to seven feet in length with an iron head and wooden stave, and shorter throwing spears. The latter was the principal ballistic weapon of the period as the longbow was regarded as a hunting implement. Round, or sometimes rectangular, wooden shields with protruding doomed or conical iron bosses, were carried by warriors of all ranks. Body armour was limited to linked iron rings threaded onto cloth or, later, loose chain mail - though some warriors fought naked. According to Julius Caesar the British Celts covered themselves in blue woad to give them a more frightening appearance in battle. [6] Tall helmets were worn, at least by the nobility, some being embellished with ridges, studs and horns.

The Celts most feared weapon was the war-chariot. Julius Caesar has left us an excellent description of these terrifying military vehicles in action. "The chariots of the Britons," wrote Caesar, "begin the fighting by charging over the battlefield. From them they hurl javelins; although the noise of the wheels and chariot teams are enough to throw any enemy into panic. The charioteers are very skilled. They can drive their teams down very steep slopes without losing control. Some warriors can run along the chariot pole, stand on the yoke and then dart back into the chariot." [7] After this impressive display the chariot teams would dismount and engage the enemy on foot. The chariots were then kept in readiness for a rapid retreat if the battle went against them.

By the start of the last century BC, Britain had become divided into a number of large tribal groupings and armed conflict was more likely to have occurred between these groups than their component parts. Yet the greatest threat to the Celts came not from their own internecine struggles but from the mightiest military force of the ancient world - the Roman Empire.

Celtic warfare was seen as an opportunity to display individual bravery and it was not unusual for battles to be decided by single combat between the champions of opposing tribes. With such a philosophy, subtle tactics and complex manoeuvres were both despised and pointless. When they faced the disciplined Roman legions they opposed them with nothing but their courage and their strength.

Julius Caesar's two early campaigns against Briton were little more than extended raids designed to intimidate the tribes who were giving support to the Celtic Gauls in their war against Rome. But his military victories enabled him to impose restrictions upon the Celtic leaders which guaranteed a degree of stability in Britain. The principal British chieftain at this time was Cunobelin, the ruler of the Catuvellauni tribe that occupied the Thames Basin. Cunobelin appears to have generally complied with Caesar's impositions but upon his death his sons, Togodmunus and Caratacus, in violation of Caesar's treaties, moved against the Celts of the Sussex region, a Belgic tribe known as the Atrebates. The Atrebates had invaded Sussex four years after Julius Caesar's second British campaign. They were led at the time of their occupation of Sussex by Commius who was strongly pro-Roman.

The Catuvellauni drove the Atrebates southwards until they were left clinging to the Sussex coast and the new Atrebatic leader, Verica, sought refuge in Gaul - appealing to Rome for assistance. It is possible that during this time, when the Atrebates were being hard-pressed by the Catuvellauni, that a series of defensive dykes were created to the north of Chichester. Now known as the Chichester Dykes (or the Devil's Ditches) these once-considerable earthworks form a discontinuous line over ten kilometres long. The Lavant estuary was an important inlet in early times and these dykes could well have formed the defences of the main harbour of Verica's kingdom located somewhere in the Chichester-Selsey region. It has also been suggested that the dykes were built when the Atrebates first occupied the Selsey peninsula in 50 BC and that they were a form of beach-head to protect their landing base. [8]

The unrest in Britain prompted the Romans to mount a full-scale invasion of the island under the pretext of supporting their ally Verica. This time, though, the Romans intended not merely to restore the previous order but to conquer.

In 43 AD the Emperor Claudious sent four legions across the Channel under the command of Anlus Plautius. The Britons, led by Caratacus, were decisively beaten in a battle near the River Medway and the Romans quickly subdued south-eastern Britain. Plautius then sent the Second Legion (*Legio II Augusta*), commanded by the future emperor Flavius Vespasian, southwards to form a base in preparation for the conquest of the Isle of Wight and the west country.

The most obvious place for such an encampment was at the principal Atrebatic port at the mouth of the Lavant. This site was close to the Isle of Wight, could be easily supplied by sea and was located in friendly Atrebatic territory. It is even possible that as soon as the Catuvellauni had been defeated and the Roman presence in Britain was firmly established, supplies were being shipped to the Lavant estuary in anticipation of Vespasian's arrival.

A Roman legion numbered around 5,300 men to which were added native auxiliaries - in this case quite probably revengeful, or booty-seeking, Atrebatic Celts. The legion was divided into *cohorts*. The No.1 cohort was a crack fighting unit of 800 men, the other cohorts numbering only 480. Each cohort was split into *centuries* of originally 100 men, but by this date nearer eighty, under the command of a *centurion*. Centuries were composed of ten sub-units called *conturbernia* of eight to ten legionaries each.

Legionaries were armed with two seven feet long javelins (or *pila*) which had an effective throwing range of thirty yards. They were made with a thin iron shaft which bent on impact with a solid object. If the pila struck the shield of an enemy the weapon would bury itself into the shield and then buckle. The bent pila could not be removed easily from the shield which now had a seven feet long iron pole hanging from it. Inevitably, in the heat of battle, the shield would be quickly discarded. The Legionaries would then move in upon the shield-less enemy and finish them off with their swords.

Legionaries were heavily armoured with metal plates on the chest, back and across the shoulders, all three plates being held together with leather straps. Below this was a skirt of leather and metal throngs and, above, a bronze or iron helmet. His defensive armour was completed by a large, convex, rectangular shield.

The legion was an infantry formation. Its cavalry arm was formed from the native auxiliaries. These were armed with both spears and swords. Flat, oval or hexagonal shields were also carried. The auxiliaries also provided small cohorts of light infantry, a contingent of archers and even some troops armed with slings.

Roman field artillery consisted of *catapultae* and *cheiroballistae*. The former were huge bows which were tensioned by handspikes and could propel a javelin 1,000 yards. The ballistae was a spring-loaded gun that fired foot-long metal bolts. It has been stated that the Second Legion may have had as many as sixty ballistae and used them to great effect against the Britons.

It has been estimated that Vespasian commanded between 8-10,000 men. His camp on the Lavant estuary was therefore of a considerable size with a well-palisaded earthen perimeter and wooden barracks. The legion moved off from the camp to seize the Isle of Wight around 44-5 AD. The Second Legion is known to have fought a number of battles and to have taken twenty British strongholds. Though most of these engagements were against the Belgae and Durotriges of Hampshire and Dorset, it is possible, that Flavious' march through Catuvellaunian-held territory in Sussex was not without incident. It is certainly possible that they met some opposition at Mount Caburn where Roman scabbards have been found next to the charred remains of the fort's wooden gateway.

The camp on the Lavant estuary continued as an important Roman base and the harbour, with its associated buildings, began to take on a more permanent appearance. But it was not

The ramparts and ditch that are typical of a Downland hillfort. This photograph is of Mount Caburn which can be reached by foot from Glynde, (TQ 445089).

until the second century that the town of Noviomagus Regentium was properly fortified. Running for one and a half miles, the original walls were made of earth faced with flint and mortar. In the third century these were replaced with massive stone walls, the foundations of which still encompass the centre of what we now call Chichester.

The Roman policy of allowing local chieftains to remain in power in their own provinces was extended to Britain. Though they adopted Latin names, wore Roman robes and lived in luxurious villas, these leaders were still Celts. After the occupation of the south-east the Celt Cogidubnus was installed as the client king of the area previously ruled by Verica. His capital was Noviomagus Regentium.

Noviomagus means 'newmarket' and the place became an important commercial centre. From its once-mighty walls the famous Stane Street began its long journey to London, bisecting the dense forests of the Weald. At some time in the fourth century, probably after AD 367 when Barbarian raids against the English coast increased, bastions were added to the city walls. The bastions were built to house ballistae. Around the entire defensive perimeter a deep and wide ditch was also dug. To serve the ballistae Chichester must have maintained a permanent garrison.

Barbaric simplicity gave way to Romanesque sophistication and for almost four hundred years peace reigned throughout most of present day England. Yet the grandeur that was Rome proved too tempting a prize to both barbarian and citizen. Pax Romana could not be sustained. Internal divisions and external assault led to the Roman legions being withdrawn from Britannica. Attacks from the Germanic nations of northern Europe led to the development of defensive works along the coast of southern Britain.

A series of forts, each protecting a good harbour, was built from Norfolk to the Isle of Wight. Under the command of a Count of the Saxon Shore, the walled city of Chichester and the great fort at Pevensey (Anderida) **formed part of a defensive network designed to repel the** barbarian hordes. 9

The east gateway of the Roman Saxon Shore fort of Anderida at Pevensey.

Chichester's "Palace" bastion in the south-west quadrant of the city. The bastion can be seen from the "Walls Walk" which is accessible from numerous points around the city, (SU 858045).

Chichester was merely a fortified city but Pevensey was a purpose-built military fortification. Encompassing some nine acres of land the fort's irregular oval trace followed the line of what was once a promontory that reached out into the sea. It had walls thirty feet high linked to ten bastions. Each, no doubt, mounted a great catapultae or ballistae.

With the withdrawal of the last Roman legions in 410 the Emperor Honorius wrote to the British towns and told them that they would now be responsible for their own defence. In 367 the country had suffered from attacks by the Picts, Scots, Francs and Saxons acting in concert in what has become known as "the great barbarian conspiracy". [10] To help combat the barbarian hordes the Britons introduced mercenaries from the Continent to defend the Saxon Shore. Pevensey Fort, for example, was garrisoned by warriors of unknown origin called the Abulci.[11] The defences of the Saxon Shore proved inadequate, however, and the Germanic invasions of Britain began.

2
South Saxons
A County Created

To counter the barbarian incursions of the 5th century it is believed that Ambrosius Aurelianus, High King of the Britons, erected what has been called the Ambrosian barrier around the south-eastern coastline. This possibly took no more than the form of concentrations of troops to defend a particular area. It has been proposed that these points can be identified by the prefix Amb. Thus at Amberley, Ambersham and possibly Amberstone (near Pevensey Castle) were established the most southerly garrisons of the Ambrosian barrier. [1]

Despite these precautions the Saxons crossed the Channel in three ships landing at a place called Cymensora in the year 477. They were led by Aelle and his three sons, Cymen, Wlencing and Cyssa (or Cissa). It would seem that the landing was opposed by the Britons - to the Saxons they were simply Welsh, or foreigners - many of whom were killed and the rest driven into the Weald (the Andresweald). Cymensora is believed to have been near Selsey but the reference in the *Anglo-Saxon Chronicles* to the Britons retreating into the Weald would indicate that Aelle's landing was further to the east and it is certainly possible that Aelle landed somewhere between the Arun and the Cuckmere rivers. [2]

The Saxon's first objective would have been Noviomagus. By this time the city was slipping into ruin, though it was still the most important urban centre in the region. Cissa later rebuilt the city which became Cissa-ceaster and eventually Chichester. It is possible that the old British hill forts, particularly Cissbury Ring (Cissbury means 'Cissa's fort') and Mount Caburn, were reoccupied at this time by the Britons.

Over the course of the next thirteen years the Saxons consolidated their position and extended their territory eastwards, though it would seem that the Ambrosian barrier restricted the invaders to the coastal plain. It is known that they fought at least one battle by the unidentified 'Mearcredes' stream. Rivers have always been of considerable tactical importance and a fight at a river crossing was typical of the warfare of the period. This battle was fought, almost certainly, on the banks of either the Arun, the Adur or the Ouse. Whilst at least one authority states that this encounter took place at Seaford near the Ouse, local tradition tells us that the Britons clashed, unsuccessfully, at Slonk Hill to the north-east of Shoreham. The origin of the word 'slonk' is found in the Saxon word for slaughter. Thus Slonk Hill is slaughter hill. Yet Slonk Hill is not defensible and if the Britons did attempt to stem the Saxon advance the more likely battlefield would be the adjoining Mill Hill which overlooks the River Adur, possibly the Mearcredesburna of Anglo-Saxon tradition. Certainly the large number of Saxon burial sites between Shoreham and Pevensey may indicate that the invaders encountered stiff resistance from the Britons throughout this area. [3]

At Slonk Hill the invaders were successful and they continued eastwards until they reached the Roman fort at Pevensey (the fort of Anderida). Here Aelle and Cyssa stormed the defences and, according to *The Anglo-Saxon Chronical*, "killed all who were inside, so there was not one Briton left." This was no easy victory for the Saxons. According to a twelfth century writer, Henry of Huntigdon, the fort was besieged for many days with the Saxons finding themselves under attack by the natives using the Andresweald as cover from which they mounted hit-and-run raids. The invaders were only able to take the fort when they divided their forces in two - one to keep the British guerrillas at bay, the other to assault the walls.

The capture of Pevensey is recorded in the year 491 AD though dates in the early pages of the *Chronical* are unreliable. [4]

The territory conquered by Alle and his sons became known as Suthseaxe which means the South Saxons. In time Suthseaxe became Sussex. Aelle himself became the leader of all the Germanic tribes south of the Humber and the first man to carry the title of *Bretwaldas* (Broad-Wielder), or High King of the English.

The Germanic invasion, which had swept across eastern and southern Britain, encountered a determined resistance in the west in the form of the legendary British warrior, Arthur. Though evidence of Arthur's existence is scanty, what is quite certain is that the Saxon advance was met with great force. It was against this force that Aelle led a confederation of Anglo-Saxons from Sussex and Kent.

The opposing armies clashed at Mount Baden (Mons Badonicus) which is possibly somewhere to the north of Bath. For three days battle raged with Arthur and his Britons achieving a momentous victory. Aelle's defeat was so complete that the Saxon conquest of Britain was halted and for the next seventy years the invaders were left in occupation of only East Anglia, Kent and a narrow strip along the Sussex and Hampshire coasts.

Gradually, however, the whole of the Sussex area came under Saxon control. This was probably through a process of confrontation rather than integration as there are few place names in Sussex that are of Celtic origin. Strung out in their small communities along the Downs and the edges of the Weald, the Britons would stand little chance against the organised Saxon forces.

It would seem that the marsh land to the west of Pevensey marked the limit of the South Saxon's domain. Beyond this area, in and around present-day Hastings, a separate Germanic group, the Haestingas, maintained an independent existence until they were conquered by Offa of Mercia in 771.

From the archaeological and pictorial evidence available it has been concluded that the weapons, and therefore the tactics, employed by the Britons and the Saxons were largely the same.

The relative scarcity of swords and hand-axes amongst the British and the Anglo-Saxons may indicate that these weapons were the preserve of the nobility, and the word Saxon was probably derived from the Seax, a single-edged, long dagger (about eighteen inches) carried by the Saxons. Saxon body armour was usually no more than a thick leather jerkin and helmets do not seem to have been worn.

Warfare at this time was conducted at close quarters. The Saxons fought almost exclusively on foot with their shields

Two drum towers and a section of the walls of the medieval castle at Pevensey.

An aerial view of the Roman fort of Anderida, with the medieval castle of Pevensey occupying its south-eastern corner.
(By kind permission of English Heritage and Skyscan Photography).

Wulfnoth to destroy the stranded vessels. Though it would seem that with this victory Wulfnoth won his way back into royal favour, the loss of ships was disastrous for England, allowing the Danes to raid the length of the south coast. Finally, in 1017, the last of the great Wessex kings of the Saxons, Edmund Ironside, died. With his demise all resistance to the Danes ended, and the Danish leader, Cnut, was acknowledged King of England.

For over twenty years the Danes ruled England until the sudden death of Cnut's son Harthacnut left the throne vacant. A protracted, though bloodless, power struggle resulted in the restoration of Alfred's royal line in the form of Edward the Confessor. Edward's accession brought together all the feuding elements as his father (Ethelred the Unread) was English and his mother, Emma of Normandy, had also married Cnut the Dane.[14]

Edward had lived in his mother's country for most of his life and he continued to maintain his connections with the Normans. Though nominally part of France, Normandy was, in fact, an independent Nordic country, it's territory having been won from the French in the late 9th century.

A few years after his assumption of the throne Edward invited his friend William, Duke of Normandy, to England. It may have been during this visit that Edward promised William that he would succeed him as King of England. William, as Edward's cousin once-removed, through his great-aunt Queen Emma, was the closest adult male relative to The Confessor and, arguably, the rightful heir to the English throne.

At this time another famous figure first makes his appearance upon History's stage. Harold Godwin (or Godwinson), Earl of Wessex, was Edward's most powerful subject and the country's leading military commander having beaten the Welsh and extended Edward's rule into south Wales. From comparatively obscure origins Harold's father (who was probably of English descent, possibly the son of Wulfnoth Cild) married into a branch of the Danish royal family and in time became one of Cnut's most trusted subordinates. When Edward became king, Godwin, as Earl of Wessex, established himself as the unrivalled

power behind the throne. His relationship with Edward was a stormy one which reached a head in 1048 when Godwin openly defied the king.

One of Edward's Norman friends, Eustace of Boulogne, was returning to France from a visit to London when he entered Dover and demanded accommodation for himself and his entourage. One of the townsfolk refused to admit an armed foreigner into his house and a fight broke out. Others became involved and at the end of the dispute nineteen Normans and twenty English lay dead.

Eustace demanded retribution and, as Dover fell within Godwin's domains, Edward ordered Godwin to punish the townspeople. Godwin, quite understandably, refused and the enraged Edward banished Godwin from his kingdom.

Godwin was now seen as the champion of the English and when a year later he returned to England and sailed along the shores of his old earldom he gathered considerable support at Pevensey, Hastings and along the Kent coast. The strength of Godwin's force compelled Edward to reconsider his support for the Normans and all Godwin's previous rights, lands and privileges were restored.

Shortly after his showdown with Edward, Godwin died and his eldest son Harold took not only his father's title of Earl of Wessex but also his position as Edward's chief advisor. As the years passed Edward's participation in government decreased and the affairs of state were administered almost entirely by Harold who was given more titles and greater authority. At one time the Godwin family held four of the five largest earldoms in England but two of Harold's brothers disgraced themselves - Tostic and Sweyn - and they were driven into exile. This could not have happened without Harold's authorisation and it turned Tostic into a bitter enemy.

In 1064 Harold set off by ship from Bosham harbour near Chichester. His destination and his reasons for travelling have never been satisfactorily established but strong winds blew his ship along the French coast to Ponthieu where Harold and his retinue were captured and imprisoned.

Duke William managed to secure Harold's release from the Count of Ponthieu and made him welcome at his palace at Rouen. During his stay in Normandy Harold fought with the Norman army in an attack against Brittany and in return was knighted by William. It was later recorded in the text accompanying the Bayeux Tapestry, that at this time, Harold took an oath upon some holy relics. This may therefore have implied, as William was subsequently to allege, that Harold would support the Duke's claim to the English throne in the increasingly likely event that Edward died without an heir. In response to this William confirmed Harold in his earldom and allowed him to return to England.

Whether or not Harold made such an oath, or whether it was made under duress, is not known, but as his liberty was entirely dependent upon William's goodwill, it was hardly likely that Harold could have refused such a request. Yet Harold was a commoner and he had no right to even consider himself a candidate for the English crown.

At the beginning of the fateful year of 1066 it was clear that Edward was dying. He had no obvious heir and the only legitimate contender was a distant relative who was still a child. So, on his deathbed, Edward gave his hand to Harold and, it was claimed, offered him the throne of England.

150
175
225
250
275

LONDON 64 MILES
CALDBEC HILL
350
325

LONDON 61 MILES
300
TRACK
275
250
225
200
175
150

HAROLD
ENGLISH

275 250 225 200 175

THE BATTLE OF HASTINGS 1066

200
Heights in feet
0   200   400   600
Yards
0   200   400   600
Metres

Streams to River Brede   175
175
175

TRACK
125
150
175
200
225
250
275

FRENCH

NORMANS

BRETONS

TELHAM HILL 300

TRACK

Streams to Bulverhythe

HASTINGS 5 MILES

125 125   125   150   175   200 225

275

250

22

3
Conquers and Castles
The Battle of Hastings

On the night of 4 January 1066, Edward the Confessor died. The following morning he was buried at the new abbey of West Minster. Edward had personally planned and supervised the construction of the great building and he was the first man to be interned within its walls. That same afternoon Harold Godwin was crowned King of England in the same building. Though his succession was endorsed by the *Witan*, the embryonic Saxon parliament, others were to dispute his claim and Harold must have known that he would have to fight to keep his crown.

Harold's claim to the throne, apart from Edward's deathbed endorsement, was based on the fact that his father had married the sister of Ulf who was Cnut's brother-in-law. Edward's Queen Emma was also Harold's sister. If these tenuous links with the Danish and English royal lines were justification for Harold's succession then Harold's younger brother Tostig, the recently disgraced and exiled Earl of Northumberland, also had a claim. So too did Ulf's son Svein, King of Denmark, as did Duke Willliam of Normandy whose mother Emma had married that great warrior Cnut and to whom Edward may have once promised the English throne. The Norwegian king, Harald Hardrada, also cast his eyes across the North Sea. The Vikings had a long record of successful attacks upon England and many people of Norwegian descent had settled in the north-east of the country where he might attract some support.

Fortunately for Harold, Svein, who was Harold's cousin and friend, did not press his claim. But Tostig immediately began to canvas for support and William made preparations to invade England and claim what he genuinely seemed to believe was his rightful inheritance.

England had proven to be vulnerable to the Viking raids of previous generations and its reputation as a fighting nation cannot have been high. But it was no mere raid that William of Normandy proposed to his barons when they met the Duke in the castle of Lillabonne at the beginning of spring. He planned to attack and subjugate an entire country, a country far larger than his own. Such an operation would require a huge army and a massive fleet to transport it across the perilous waters of the Channel. William had neither and it was obvious that he would need assistance from outside Normandy.

If the Duke was to persuade enough men to join his adventure he would have to convince them that such an enterprise would succeed. Yet the scale of the operation and the obstacles that stood in William's way were unprecedented. Not since Caesar, a thousand years earlier, had a general attempted to transport an entire army across the Channel. It would be almost another thousand years before such an enterprise would be repeated when the Allies invaded Normandy in 1944, and that was the single largest combined military, naval and air operation ever mounted.

Though William's barons had little choice but to offer their backing, without the approval of his overlord, the King of France, he could not leave his territory unprotected. So, following the meeting at Lillabonne, William rode to the great capitals of western and northern France to garner support for his expedition and assurances from his rivals that they would not attack Normandy in his absence. A deputation was also sent to Rome where the Pope was persuaded to condemn Harold for breaking his sacred oath and to sanction William's claim to the English throne. This was a critical decision as William could now seize the moral high ground. The Witan may have chosen Harold but William had been selected by a higher authority - by God.

Despite the obvious perils of the proposed invasion, with the offer of estates and titles to those men who would follow him, William soon found plenty of ambitious knights prepared to join his growing army, especially since he had received papal approval. From as far north as Flanders and as far south as Italy they flocked into Normandy to join William's great enterprise. Men he now had, but his greatest problem was transportation. No-one had ever tried to ship a medieval army such a distance (from the harbour at Dives to the English coast is approximately ninety to ninety-five nautical miles) and it was clear that he would need to build hundreds of vessels, and that would take time.

Time, by contrast, was exactly what Harold did not need. As early as April, Tostig, possibly in collusion with William, had crossed the Channel with some sixty ships and had raided the coastal settlements of Sussex and Kent. Harold called out his forces but his brother then sailed up the east coast, no doubt hoping to draw Harold away from the south. The new king of England was not deceived. Tostig's force was small and could be left safely to the fyrd of Mercia and Northumbria.[1] The real danger had yet to materialise.

Harold was fully aware that William intended to invade as he had received a number of threatening letters from the angry Duke. The English king had assembled a large force of infantry and his entire fleet of around 400 ships at the Isle of Wight. All summer long he waited for the Normans to appear. The prevailing winds in the Channel throughout the summer months blow from the south-west and any invasion force from Normandy would be carried by these winds to the beaches of Sussex and Kent. By placing his fleet at the Isle of Wight those same winds would sweep Harold down the coast and upon the rear of the invaders. Harold had called out the fyrd to defend their country and his force on the Isle of Wight amounted to around 10,000 men with other warriors watching the tides along the coast. Their obligatory military service was two months each year, and for more than eight weeks the men of the fyrd had waited with growing impatience for the threatened attack. At some point Harold would have to allow his troops to return home but soon it would be autumn and then winter when no invader would dare put to sea.

By early August William was ready. He had put together a huge fleet in the harbour at the mouth of the River Dives. It is impossible to know how many ships William may have had. Figures in early accounts range from 696 to 11,000 vessels and between 10,000 and 60,000 men. As William fought at Hastings with approximately 8,000 men historians have estimated that the Franco-Norman fleet could have been no larger than that of the English and probably little more than 350 strong.

Their armies assembled, the two great men waited on their respective sides of the Channel for the wind that would carry them both to the shingle beaches of Sussex. The Norman ships, clearly defined in the Bayeux Tapestry, had long, shallow keels and single masts bearing a square sail. Such vessels would have limited ability to sail to windward and their shallow keels would have little effect in preventing leeway. William therefore had no choice but to wait for the wind to blow from the south or the south-west.

Meanwhile, Tostig, after suffering a heavy defeat in Lincolnshire, continued up the east coast to Scotland. Though Tostig probably appreciated that he would never be able to command enough support in England to seize power for himself, he seems to have persuaded the Scottish king, Malcolm, and then the Norwegian king, Hardrada, to join him in an attempt to invade northern England. It is possible that Tostig hoped to recover at least part of the Northumbrian earldom from which he had been banished. Malcolm, no doubt, saw an opportunity to annex territory around the English border and Hardrada must have wished to emulate the achievements of the great Viking warrior-kings of the past.

Back in Normandy, the great fleet at last set sail from Dives-sur-Mer on 12 September, but strong westerly winds blew the ships along the Norman coast. Some ships were lost and a number of men were drowned. The invasion fleet found shelter at St. Valéry in the Somme estuary more than 250 kilometres to the east of Dives. William buried his dead (in secret, presumably so as not to dishearten the rest of the troops) and waited again for a favourable wind. But the wind blew from the north and running with that wind was a dreaded old enemy. Accompanied by Harold's embittered brother Tostig came the Vikings and the most fearsome warrior of his age, Harald Hardarda.

It was now the middle of September and with the onset of the northern gales Harold dismissed the fyrd. The invasion season was over for the year and the Anglo-Saxon warriors returned to their homes and their farms. Harold, who was a Sussex man, went to his family home at Bosham for a few days before riding with his household troops back to London, only to learn that the Norsemen had landed in Northumbria.

Harold collected as many of his men as he could muster and started for the north. The English army marched 190 miles from London to York in just four days. This was a considerable achievement but it must not be assumed, as many have, that the journey was made on foot. The Anglo-Saxons, from Alfred the Great to the Duke of Wellington, have excelled as infantry and Harold's army was no different. But the men that accompanied Harold were men of rank and paid retainers. These were elite troops, not foot-sloggers. They would have ridden to York. The English despised the horse in war as it was too easy for cavalry to escape the terrifying slaughter of a medieval battlefield. The Anglo-Saxons stood and fought. The horse was seen as a means of transportation and it was on horseback that Harold travelled from London to York.

Harold and Tostig had landed at Riccall and advanced towards York, the great capital of the north. A combined force raised by the northern English earls marched from York to meet the invaders and the opposing armies clashed just outside York on 20 September at Gate Fulford, which is now a suburb of the city. Here the English were soundly beaten and the two earls, Edwin of Mercia and Morcar of Northumbria, made peace with Hardrada.

Meanwhile Harold Godwin had reached Tadcaster, less than ten miles from York, on 24 September. There he rested overnight and early the following morning he marched through York and fell upon the unsuspecting Vikings. At Stamford Bridge, ten miles beyond York, Saxons and Vikings stood toe to toe and swung their battle-axes and swords in mortal conflict. The invaders had been taken completely by surprise and many of the Norsemen had been caught without their shields and swords. The invaders were pushed back to their longboats after suffering terrible losses. Tostig was killed and Hardarda was shot through the throat by an arrow. It is said that the Norsemen sailed to England in 300 ships yet they needed only 25 of those ships to take the survivors back to Norway.

Harold had earned a remarkable victory against an enemy force probably larger than the one that William had assembled in Normandy. It was not often that an English army defeated a Norwegian horde but the invaders were so decisively beaten that never again would the Vikings threaten the shores of England. If it's memory had not been overshadowed by the events that followed, the Battle of Stamford Bridge would have been regarded as the greatest victory ever achieved by the English Saxons. So with unbridled confidence, though diminished numbers, the Anglo-Saxon army marched back to the south because the wind had changed in the Channel and William of Normandy had landed at Pevensey Bay!

Instead of entering London in triumph, Harold went to Waltham Abbey to contemplate and to consider his next move. We can only guess at his state of mind at this time. After his great victory against the Vikings did he consider himself invincible or, after two weeks of marching and fighting, was the news of the Franco-Norman invasion a crushing blow to Harold's belief in his right to the throne?

Harold knew that he would have to fight again but his men were exhausted. The most prudent policy open to Harold was for him to find a defensive position near to London and allow his troops a few more days to recuperate. William would have no choice but to march upon London where he would find the English army rested and ready for battle, supported by the population of the nation's capital. Instead Harold committed a fatal blunder and decided to drive his warriors forward again. Without even waiting for the troops of the northern earls which were already marching southwards, Harold set off from London on 12 October. With just his paid retainers and men of the London fyrd - possibly as few as 5,000 men - Harold crossed the Thames and rode down to Rochester and through the Weald. The Sussex and Kent fryd were told to join Harold's force at a well-known point on the Wealden Hills where the districts of Baldeslow, Ninfield and Hailesaltede met - the place of the Hoar (grey) Apple Tree on Caldbec Hill. To this place most, if not all, of the fighting men of Sussex must have made their way to do battle for their king.

William's fleet had sailed from the harbour of St Valéry-sur-Somme on 27 September, making landfall at around 09:00 the following morning at what is now called Norman's Bay. His force was composed of possibly 3,000 mounted knights, 1,000 archers and 4,000 foot soldiers. William's great achievement, from a military standpoint, was in crossing the Channel with such a large body of cavalry. No medieval commander had dared attempt such an operation. But the mounted troops were the flower of the Norman army and William had to take them with him if he was to have any chance of success. In the end, it would be these men that would tip the scales of victory in favour of the invaders. Armed with lances and long, heavy swords or iron maces, the cavalry were protected from neck to knee in chain mail, their heads covered with iron helmets and nose-guards. Long, tapering shields were also carried. The comparatively recent introduction of the stirrup had increased the fighting effectiveness of the mounted soldier considerably. Not only did the stirrup give the rider a more secure seat and greater control of his mount, it also enabled him to get the full weight of his body behind his lance when charging an enemy and when striking at an opponent with a sword or mace. With the aid of this simple invention the mounted knight would dominate European warfare for much of the Middle Ages. The Norman infantry, being of lower rank, were not so heavily armed and some may have carried just a single weapon, be it either sword or spear. Many of the archers wore neither protective mail nor helmets.

William must have expected his landing to be opposed by the English and his disembarkation was conducted in true military fashion, as Robert Wace explained just 100 years later: "The archers were the first to land, each with his bow bent and his quiver full of arrows slung at his side ... The knights landed next, all armed, with their hauberks on, their shields slung at their necks and their helmets laced." [2] Shortly after landing William, with an escort of just twenty-five men, including William fitzObern one of his key military advisors, undertook a reconnaissance of the area.

The Normans immediately erected a wooden fort within the confines of Pevensey castle. It has been suggested that the wood was brought from Normandy already pre-cut so that the walls could be assembled very quickly. His beach-head thus secured, William waited for the attack that he believed was imminent. But Harold was still moving down to London from Yorkshire and it was at least two weeks after the Normans had landed that the English army assembled on the High Weald. Whilst they waited for Harold's force to appear, the invaders moved along the coast to Hastings, scavenging for food and ransacking many of the villages between Pevensey and Hastings on the way. At Hastings William ordered another castle to be built, this time using conscripted local labour. William could not leave the coast to seek out Harold. He did not have any idea where the English might be and every step that he took further inland took him deeper into hostile territory. Also, and of over-riding importance, was the fact that he dare not leave his fleet unprotected for fear that it could be captured or destroyed.

Whilst they waited, the Normans plundered the region around Hastings. This may simply have been the troops foraging for supplies to keep the army and its horses fed. It has also been suggested that the Normans undertook such destruction in order to induce Harold to move against them immediately, for the longer that they remained in one place the more difficult it would become for them to find food in the area. Sussex was part of Harold's hereditary earldom of Wessex and he could hardly remain inactive whilst his people and their homes were being destroyed. In fact the ravaging of the countryside was one of William's principle tactics and one that he had employed previously to great effect, particularly in 1063 when William had successfully attacked Maine.[3]

Such actions were commonplace in medieval Europe and it had led to the building of castles throughout the Continent. Before the advent of gunpowder and the introduction of heavy ordnance into siege warfare, the walls of stone castles were extremely difficult to breach. Faced with invasion, the defending forces could retire into the safety of their castles. The invaders would be free to harry the countryside but they would not be able to settle in the invaded land because the defending army would still be intact and able to counter-attack as, and when, the opportunity presented itself. It was said by Oderic Vitalis [4] that the English were severely disadvantaged by the lack of stone-built fortifications and this view was confirmed by the fact that the Normans began building castles from the day that they landed.

The prospect of plunder would attract large numbers of men to join the army of a successful commander. Though some of William's supporters had been promised great estates, not all of his men could be given land. Many must have followed William just for the chance of unlicensed rape and pillage. Yet, if William of Malmesbury is to be believed,[5] Harold did not share out the spoils of war after the victory at Stamford Bridge and as a result few men, other than his household troops, followed him south to face the Normans. This could possibly explain why Harold, King of a large and well-populated country, faced William with only a few thousand soldiers. It may well be that Harold had sealed his fate at Hastings with that decision at Stamford Bridge.

At last, on 13 October 1066, the English army could be seen gathering on Caldbec Hill, some five miles to the north-west of Hastings. In a campaign of this nature, in relatively unknown territory, early warning of the approach of the enemy was crucial to the invaders and William's cavalry scouts were clearly pushed far and wide. The sudden and rapid approach of the English caused William to withdraw his foraging parties and advanced pickets and he concentrated his army in readiness for an immediate onslaught by Harold. Throughout the night of the 13th, the Normans, fearing a surprise attack, stood to arms. At this time William also learnt that Harold had sent his fleet round the coast to cut off the Norman's retreat and prevent any reinforcements being sent from France.

Some historians have criticised Harold for concentrating his army too close to the Norman encampment. Yet his position was ideal for defence and was near enough to the Norman camp to force William to attack without delay. It is also possible that Harold had hoped to attack the Normans and catch them unprepared as he had caught the Vikings at Stamford Bridge. But William's cavalry pickets had spotted the English army approaching across the Weald. The similarities in Harold's march to Tadcaster and his march to Caldbec Hill could also support the view that Harold hoped to surprise William as he had Tostic and Hardrada.

The subject of the English deployment is one of considerable interest. At some point in time, possibly on the morning of the 14th, Harold moved southwards from Caldbec Hill down to Senlac Hill (also now known as Battle Hill). Why this movement occurred is not known. It may have been that Harold, having assembled his forces on Caldbec Hill, was continuing his advance upon Hastings and that the only reason why he stopped on the Senlac ridge was because he had seen the Normans marching to meet him. It has been stated that the vanguard of William's army spotted the English coming out of the woods on Caldbec Hill and emerging onto the Senlac ridge that crossed the Hastings road.

Such statements have led some to claim that Harold was taken by surprise and his men were still taking up their positions when the Normans began their attack. It is certainly difficult to understand why Harold moved from Caldbec Hill if he intended to fight a defensive battle. Caldbec Hill, at 300 feet above sea level, is higher than Senlac Hill and its sides are steeper. Harold had already rejected the suggestions of his advisors to remain on the defensive at London and wait for William to attack him. Therefore it seems extraordinary that Harold would march so purposely - without waiting for the northern earls to join him - all the way from London just to take up a defensive position near Hastings.

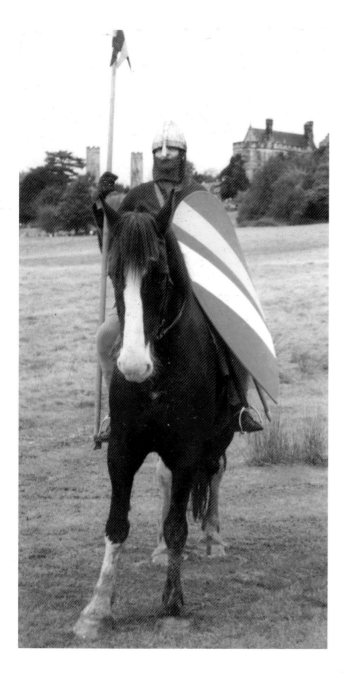

A Norman knight waits at the foot of Senlac Hill.
In the background are the remains of Battle Abbey where Harold's army stood. The battlefield of Hastings is part of the English Heritage property of Battle Abbey, Battle, (TQ 448001).

It has been stated by some historians that Harold took up a defensive position on Caldbec Hill whilst he awaited the reinforcements which he knew would reach him in a day or two. Indeed, one chronicler claimed that by the 13th Harold still had only one-third of the total force that he expected would eventually join him. [6]

It is more likely that Harold planned to attack the Normans and take them by surprise - as he had the Vikings - but when he saw thousands of mounted knights approaching at the head of William's army he realised that he could not operate in open order against such a large body of cavalry. He took advantage of the terrain and assembled his force upon Senlac Hill. No other course of action fits the known facts.

There are no accurate records to tell us the size of the English army. Military experts have examined Harold's position and they have estimated that, standing shoulder to shoulder and eight men deep, no more than seven or eight thousand men could have formed a battle-line upon the Senlac Hill. In the *Chronicon ex Chronicis* of 1118, Florence of Worcester declared that many Englishmen left Harold's army before the battle because the hill was already too crowded. The English and Norman armies, therefore, were roughly the same size. It was in their composition and their tactics that the opposing forces differed.[7]

Harold's army was composed entirely of foot warriors. They carried battle-axes, swords and spears as their principle armament, with throwing axes, javelins and even stones tied to sticks as their missile weapons. There were few archers in Harold's army. It is usually stated that this was because the bow was used in England mainly for hunting and was not considered to be an instrument of war. This is not entirely true. That there were fewer English archers than Norman at the Battle of Hastings seems certain. The accounts written after the battle and the

Bayeux Tapestry all agree on this point. The bow would indeed have been used for hunting but it was also considered to be a weapon of war. It was used by the English at Stamford Bridge (Hadrada, remember, had been killed by an arrow) and it was used at Hastings. But it was seen as a weapon of the lower classes and a large part of Harold's army was composed of men of rank so the bow was not their weapon of choice. Equally, the archers that had fought so successfully at Stamford Bridge would not have been able to march from York with the mounted retainers. The forces moving down from the north to join Harold later may well have included large numbers of archers.

Though the bulk of the English army was made up of fyrdsmen the king also possessed a number of retainers that lived on the royal estates whose military duty included the provision of their own arms and horses. These were the famed housecarls. As both Earl of Wessex and King of England, Harold would have been able to support the cost of approximately 3,000 housecarls. Some of these would have fallen at Stamford Bridge and no more than 2,000 could have been present on 13 October. Harold's brothers, Gyrth and Leofwin, who held earldoms in East Anglia, Kent and Surrey, together would have been able to provide another 2,000 of their own housecarls.

This force of well-armed and well-paid professional soldiers formed the backbone of the army. Alongside these fearsome warriors stood the wealthy landowners, also well-armed. The Bayeaux Tapestry shows some of the English wearing chain mail and helmets, and these would be the thegns and housecarls but others, the fyrdsmen, appear with no armour, possessing just shields for protection

If the English were to fight a defensive battle then their tactics would be simple. From behind their shield wall the men, packed into one massed formation, would swing their mighty battle-axes and throw their javelins. If the men held their ground (and their nerve) the enemy would be unable to make much impression upon such a body in hand-to-hand combat alone.

A Norman archer on the battlefield of Hastings, at Battle.

Such tactics did not require a complex command structure. All each man had to do was stand and fight. It cannot be said that Harold directed his troops other than by personal example and they would not be capable of any manoeuvre other than a wild change. By contrast, William's army, with its large proportion of mounted troops, was an offensive force and needed careful handling. It's three arms, the bowmen, infantry and cavalry had to be organised, disciplined and controlled to be truly effective. William, therefore, split his army into three divisions. The main division, led by William himself, was entirely Norman. Of the other divisions, one was a French and Flemish force (with a small Norman contingent) under Count Eustace of Boulogne, and the other was a mixed body of mercenaries from Brittany, Anjou and Maine.

This last division was commanded by a Breton called Alan Fergant. Each division was a well-balanced force of all three arms though the centre division, under William, was possibly twice the size of the other two.

There does not seem to have been the same formal and clearly defined military structure in Normandy as the semi-feudal system of Late Saxon England. It appears to have been an ad-hoc arrangement. Individuals were granted land, or inherited land, in return for which they supplied a fully armoured and mounted knight or knights depending on the terms of the arrangement between themselves and their overlords. The length of military service each year also seems to have been arbitrary. Forty days was regarded as the usual period of time but it is likely that the men served for as long as they were required or faced penalties as a consequence.[8]

Whatever the differences, the same basic principles applied in both armies. In return for land or money the recipients fought for their lord or sovereign when ordered to do so.

At dawn on Saturday 14 October, the leading units of the Franco-Norman army marched out of Hastings. William's army was soon strung out for many miles along the narrow track that led passed the Senlac Hill on its way to join the London Road. By the middle of the morning most of William's force had assembled at the foot of Harold's position.

Running for approximately 750 yards, with a width of some 150 yards, the Senlac ridge rises steeply for some sixty feet above the foot of Telham Hill. The ground to the left of the ridge is even steeper than the main ascent and to the right, where the slope is easier, was an area of marshy ground. Behind the ridge lay part of the dense Andredsweald forest. William's options were therefore limited. His main strike force was his mounted knights and they could not operate effectively on the difficult terrain that flanked Harold's position. The Duke had no choice but to mount a frontal assault.[9] It would be a brutal battle of attrition until the English line broke.

It was stated that a wall surrounded the English position and this is usually interpreted as being the shield wall, though one historian, E. A. Freeman [10], positively asserts that this was a palisade erected around the hill. For this assertion to be true the troops, who had marched all the previous day, would have had to spend the evening cutting trees. They would also have already planned a defensive battle. Whilst neither of these actions are impossible what rules out such a supposition is that the English would already have had it in mind to fight their defensive battle on Senlac Hill, not on Calbec Hill where they spent the night. For if they prepared their palisades for use on Calbec Hill they would have had to pull them up to move forward to Senlac Hill the following morning. This simply does not make sense, nor is there any recorded evidence of it happening. The shield wall was the only wall that Harold's men stood behind.

As they came down the northern face of Telham Hill the Normans deployed into battle order to the left of the track, facing their enemy. William would not have been able to identify Harold in the midst of the English army but he could see the Dragon banner of Wessex and Harold's personal flag of The Fighting Man flying above the centre of the ridge. Defiantly, William set his standard directly opposite that of his enemy.[11]

The battle opened at around nine o'clock with a volley of

arrows from the Norman archers. They used a short bow with an effective range of around a hundred yards. It was most probably from this distance that the first volley was fired. The housecarls, forming the front ranks of the English army, raised their shields in an interlocking barrier and few arrows found their mark. Volley followed volley but the shield wall remained unbroken. With few arrows being returned by the handful of English bowmen, the Normans soon began to run out of missiles. At around 10.30 hours William called off his archers and ordered the attack.

To the cries of "Dex Aide!" (God help us!") the Normans marched up the gentle slope of Senlac Hill with the papal banner leading the way. "Out!", "Out!", "Out!", was the English war cry. Ahead of the Normans rode a man known as *Taillefer*, or Cleaver of Iron, who had received permission from William to be the man to strike the first blow. Throwing his sword into the air and catching it again, he galloped into the English line. He may have struck the first blow for William, but it cost him his life. As the Norman's approached the English line, the defenders "hurled their javelins and weapons of all sorts;" wrote Guy of Amiens, "they dealt savage blows with their axes and with stones hafted on handles".[12]

All three divisions of William's army attacked simultaneously and the clash of arms, the shouts of defiance and the screams of agony and terror, reverberated around that fatal hill. "With great vigour the [English] held those who dare attack them hand to hand and with their swords began to drive them back", wrote William of Poitiers, just seven years after the battle. "The Norman infantry turned in flight, terrified by this savage onslaught, and so did the knights from Brittany and the other auxiliaries on the left flank. Almost the whole line of the Duke fell back." [13]

As the Normans retreated, the Breton knights panicked and their horses bolted into the marshy ground to the west of the battlefield. Seeing the disorder amongst the Bretons, part of the fyrd broke formation and charged down the hill in pursuit of the fleeing Frenchmen. Whether this move was a reckless act undertaken by ill-disciplined troops overwhelmed by the excitement of battle, or was an intentional counter-attack ordered by Harold, will never be known. But it would have been difficult for Harold to transmit orders along the packed ranks on the hill and any attempt to do so would have the potential to cause confusion. It is safe, therefore, to assume that Harold told his troops to stand their ground at all costs, and nothing more.

The English charge, reckless or not, nearly won the day. In the confusion William was thrown off his horse and the Normans, thinking that their leader was dead, continued to retreat. If Harold would have followed up the retreating invaders at this moment, the entire course of English history might have been changed. But the Anglo-Saxon King failed to take advantage of the confusion in the Norman ranks and William re-mounted his horse, threw back his nasal-guard to make his presence known, and then rallied his troops. The Normans turned on their pursuers and encircled them. Unsupported and outnumbered, the valiant (or reckless) men of the fyrd were slaughtered. Harold had shown his weakness as a commander. William had shown his strengths as a man.

Both sides now re-grouped. Losses amongst the English front ranks were replaced from the rear and the Norman archers recovered all the arrows that they could find. With the shield wall still intact William decided to change tactics. Instead of a mixed infantry and cavalry attack, the second Norman assault would be made entirely on horseback.

The Duke led the mounted knights - the flower of his army - back up that blood-soaked hill. The opposing ranks hacked at each other with swords and axes in a heavy and prolonged period of action. Though Harold's two brothers Gyrth and Leofwine, were both killed, the English line held firm. In the savage fighting William had the first of three horses killed under him. According to William of Poitiers, and others, the Duke, seeing no prospect of breaking down the shield wall, faked a retreat in order to draw some of the defenders out of position. As the knights fell back down the hill, a thousand or more English warriors, despite witnessing the massacre of their comrades earlier, left the crest and chased after the Normans. At this point William ordered his knights to turn round. The English were surrounded and butchered.

A number of historians have argued that such a tactic as a feigned retreat would have been impossible for cavalry of the eleventh century to perform.[14] They believe that it would require not only a great degree of discipline but also a considerable amount of practice and even planning to accomplish such a manoeuvre in the confusion of a medieval battle. Yet this is exactly what had happened. At the battles of Arques in 1053 and Messina in 1060, Norman knights, including some of those who fought at Hastings, had indeed performed this exact tactic. It was not a new development in warfare and this manoeuvre had been known and practised in Europe by horsemen since Roman times. Furthermore, it is probable that this manoeuvre would not have been undertaken by all the Norman knights at once but by sub units which, in their feigned retreats, would have enticed small numbers of English from their positions and then cut them down. Rather than one large-scale planned general action it would be a succession of localised clashes.

It is hard to believe that the English would repeat their earlier mistake and this scene is not depicted in the Bayeux tapestry. Yet no authority has refuted the story and it is hard to understand how Harold could have been beaten unless large numbers of his troops broke formation. As William of Malmesbury quite correctly wrote: "The English ... formed an impenetrable body, which would have kept them safe that day, if the Normans had not tricked them into opening their ranks by a feigned flight."[15] The reason why the English were so easily duped was because the Anglo-Saxons were accustomed to fighting on foot and had not previously encountered a large and disciplined body of mounted knights such as they faced at Hastings.

The battle had decidedly turned in William's favour. With the destruction of the English right, the western end of the hill would no longer be held by the defenders. The shield wall would not have been extended to re-take this ground, quite the reverse was

the case. As losses mounted, so the shield wall contracted to ensure its integrity. So now the smaller body of defenders would have been concentrated into a position holding the central and eastern parts of the hill. The open western end of the hill, which has the most gentle gradient, could be climbed easily by the Norman horses, and the knights would no longer be forced to fight uphill. At last on the same level as the English, the mounted Normans could now strike down upon the defenders from the height of their saddles.

Realising this, William staged a massive assault on the English line with his entire army. The archers were ordered to fire high into the air over the head of the front ranks to assail the lighter armed troops behind the housecarls. The defenders would have responded to this by raising their shields above their heads. Though the shields would have protected the English, raising them above their heads meant exposing their bodies as well as making it more difficult for them to wield their weapons. At the same time, therefore, the Norman infantry and cavalry were to attack the front and both flanks of the English line.

The battle had now been raging for many hours, but still both sides fought with great energy. Most medieval battles lasted no more than an hour or two before one of the opposing forces broke off the engagement and retired to the safety of its own strongholds. But there was no avenue of escape for the Normans. With their ships now surrounded by the English fleet, the invaders had to win or they would certainly die. The English dare not break formation to flee because the Norman cavalry could outpace them. They had seen the fearful consequences of such action when their comrades had chased after the Norman knights only to be slaughtered. The Normans had nowhere to run and the English could not run. So the battle continued throughout the afternoon but the English line was visibly shrinking with each attack and William's troops were able to assail every part of Harold's position with ease. It must have been evident to every combatant that the English had lost too many men to hold their ground much longer. The defenders were under constant attack from all sides and it could only be a matter of time before the line was broken.

Harold could not win the battle and he should have ordered a withdrawal. There were woods to the rear of Senlac Hill which the Norman knights would have found difficult to penetrate. He still had thousands of men under his command and darkness was approaching. If he would have retreated into the woods and escaped through the night back to London, he could have formed another army from the northern forces that were marching south. But Harold stood his ground and fought on until, sometime in the late afternoon and as the light was beginning to fade, he was struck in the eye by an arrow.

Harold, we are told, [16] pulled the arrow out of his eye but the incident was spotted by the Normans and William ordered his knights to finish off the wounded King. The Normans charged the centre of the English line. It was reported that at least half the knights that tried to fight their way through the housecarls surrounding Harold were killed in the attempt but, finally, four Normans reached the weakened English monarch: "With the point of his lance, the first pierced Harold's shield and then penetrated his chest, drenching the ground with his blood," wrote Guy of Amiens, "with his sword, the second cut off his head ... the third disembowelled him with his javelin. The fourth hacked his leg off at the thigh and hurled it far away." [17] Harold's body was so badly mutilated that his lover, Edith Swan Neck, was the only one who was able to identify it after the battle.

The housecarls fought on until, at around 17:00, the English tried to escape under the cover of darkness. From the account of William of Poitiers it seems that the army did not keep together in an ordered withdrawal but it was a case of every man for himself. The Duke, again showing sound leadership, did not allow the English to re-form and he sent his knights off in pursuit. One party of knights that had ridden northwards through the woods, saw a group of housecarls on a slight rise beyond Caldbec Hill. The knights charged after the housecarls but they plunged into a hidden ravine. Many horses and men were killed in the fall, others by the housecarls who pelted them from above.

The housecarls were only driven from their position by an organised attack from Eustace of Boulogne and William himself. Eustace was wounded in the encounter and carried from the field. This ravine was later termed the Malfosse (the evil ditch) though its exact location has not been satisfactorily established.

The English army melted away into the night and William returned to the battlefield where he spent the night amongst the dead and the dying. His banner now flew above Senlac Hill on the very spot where the Royal Standard of Wessex stood only hours before.

Losses on both sides had been horrifically high, and Hastings is regarded as having been one of the bloodiest battles of the age.[18] It has been estimated that William's casualties amounted to more than thirty per cent of his original force and the English losses higher still. William's army, though victorious, was therefore much reduced in numbers. He had to hope and pray (which no doubt he did) that the English would now accept his right to the throne. Another such battle would ruin him.

Fearing a renewal of hostilities, William withdrew from the battlefield to his camp at Hastings on 16 October. He was in a perilous position in a hostile country with supplies running low. But reinforcements were being shipped from France to Dover and after an anxious week of inactivity, William marched eastwards along the coast.

At Dover William learnt that the grandson of Edward Ironside, Edgar Aethling, had been proposed as Harold's successor and London was preparing to resist the invaders. Over the course of the next few days the expected reinforcements arrived at Dover and William waited no longer. On 31 October he captured Canterbury, the ecclesiastical heart of the country, and sent a large detachment to cut off all the main routes into London. William marched with the rest of the army to Winchester, with his fleet tracking his movements along the coast to Chichester or Portsmouth, and occupied the old Wessex capital.

With London surrounded and the other two most important

An artist's impression of a wooden Norman tower, typical of those used in early motte and bailey castles. (By kind permission of the Director, Hastings Castle).

cities in the hands of the invaders, the leading English figures, including the Archbishop of Canterbury and Edgar Aethling, submitted to what they considered was the inevitable. They invited William to accept the throne. It was, as Wulfstan of Worcester remarked, "as though with Harold had fallen also the whole strength of the country".[19] William was crowned King of England on Christmas Day.

William had won his crown with the sword and with the sword he was compelled to defend it. Over the course of the next fifteen years he faced uprisings from the south-west to the north of England, including two attacks by Danish forces under Swein their king. William met every revolt with force, burning villages and destroying crops and farm implements in reprisal. It has been suggested that as many as 300,000 English died or were killed during William's reign as a result of these tactics.

A more structured form of feudalism overtook the system of rights and traditions of Saxon England. Estates were granted to William's leading followers in return for their military service. These powerful barons maintained bodies of armed retainers to enforce their authority and they built imposing castles to overawe the local population. Initially constructed in wood, many developed into huge stone structures, the earliest of which were in Sussex. As the vital bridge between London and Normandy, as well as being the ancestral home of Harold, Sussex had to be secured against revolt.

The county was divided into six districts or baronies, known as Rapes. The military and administrative centres were at Hastings, Pevensey, Lewes, Bramber, Arundel and Chichester. At these places the barons built their castles and the remains of these great Norman strongholds can still be seen.

The Norman castles were generally of a motte and bailey design. The motte was a large mound of earth upon which a tall tower, or "keep", was erected. This was where the great Lord would reside and was the last line of defence in a siege. Adjacent to the keep, or surrounding it, was an outer courtyard called the bailey which itself was protected by a strong wall. The walls of the bailey were usually within bow-shot of the keep. Ditches, both wet and dry, sometimes were dug around the base of the motte and/or around the foot of the walls of the bailey.

At Pevensey Castle, the old walls of the Roman fort formed an outer bailey within which was a medieval inner bailey. The keep was located by the eastern corner of the inner bailey and incorporated one of the Roman bastions into its construction. It was the first Norman castle built in England.

Lewes Castle, unusually, has two mottes with the bailey standing between them. Raised in 1069-70 by William's chief judiciar, Guliemus de Warrenne, the castle was protected by earthworks and a moat.

Overlooking the River Adur at Bramber, a castle was erected in the 1070s. The bailey was formed on top of a natural knoll and was originally surrounded by a wooden palisade. Situated in the middle of the bailey, the motte was raised to about forty feet above the courtyard. Early in the twelfth century the palisade was replaced by a stone curtain wall. Later in the century another level was added to the gatehouse to create a tall gatehouse-tower.

William built a wooden castle at Hastings, possibly from pre-fabricated parts, when he arrived there after abandoning his beach-head at Pevensey. It is possible that this was built on the shore. In the twelfth century Hastings received a great tower and bailey on the cliffs above the town.

A motte castle was raised above the banks of the River Arun

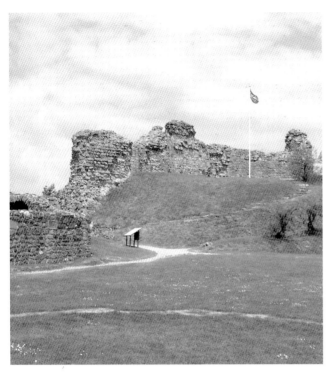

The motte and part of the east wall of Hastings Castle. The castle is on the cliffs above the town and can be reached by car via Castle Hill Road or on foot from the West Hill lift, (TQ 822094). (By kind permission of the Director, Hastings Castle).

Downs and it was located adjacent to the boundary between the Rapes of Lewes and Bramber.[20] There is no indication that its original wooden walls were ever re-built in stone.

Other Norman castles were built at Isfield in a bend of the River Uck, at Sedgwick to the east of Horsham, Pulborough, Hartfield, at Selham by the western River Rother and on St. Anne's hill close to the same river.

The Battle of Hastings was, arguably, the single most important battle in the history of mankind. Unlike many great battles, the results of this one engagement were decisive and

The ruins of the Collegiate Church and the north wall of Hastings Castle. (By kind permission of the Director, Hastings Castle).

in 1088 at Arundel, with an elevated bailey formed on either side of the motte. A stone shell keep with a crenellated parapet was added in the late twelfth century.

At Chichester, Roger de Montgomery, one of William's principle supporters, built a motte castle by the north gate of the old Roman walls. It was demolished in the early thirteenth century.

Other castles of lesser importance were raised by the Normans to help hold down the countryside. At Fulking a small motte and bailey castle was built overlooking the Weald. It commanded the underhill road that ran along the foot of the enduring. The ruling class of one nation became the rulers of another, independent, country and they occupied it permanently.

It also brought an introverted race that had been the subject of successive waves of invasion into the mainstream of western Europe. For hundreds of years after Hastings the kings of England were the overlords of Normandy and much of France. The invaded became the invaders until their empire stretched around the globe.

On 14 October 1066 a new nation was born, one that eventually became the greatest power in the world.

4
Democracy's Dawn
The Battle of Lewes

On his death William the Conqueror bequeathed England to his first son William Rufus, and Normandy to his second son Robert. This division of territory led to much dissatisfaction as many of the English barons also held property in Normandy and in 1088 there was an attempt to install Robert on the English throne. Supporters of Robert occupied Pevensey Castle as a base for another invasion from Normandy. William Rufus responded by laying siege to the castle. Pevensey's strong walls resisted every assault but, after six weeks, the defenders were starved into surrender.

When William Rufus was mysteriously killed whilst hunting in the New Forest, the Conqueror's youngest son Henry - who had not inherited any land from his father - ascended to the English throne. Again Robert threatened to assert his claim to the English crown and Henry I spent the summer of 1101 at Pevensey Castle in anticipation of an attack from across the Channel.

The tussle for the English crown was revived after the death of Henry and Pevensey was drawn into the conflict between King Stephen and Henry's daughter, Matilda. Gilbert de Clare, Earl of Pembroke, possessed Pevensey at this time and in 1147 he declared for Matilda. Pevensey Castle found itself under siege yet again. As in 1088 the castle was blockaded from both land and sea but it could not be taken by assault. Eventually, the garrison was compelled to give up the castle to the king and it remained in royal hands until 1230. Stephen also blockaded Arundel Castle in 1139 where Matilda had taken refuge but the strength of its walls deterred him from an attack and the castle was not taken.

Following Stephen's death the English and Norman territories again became united under Henry II and when the young King married Eleanor of Aquitaine, the Anglo-Norman empire extended from the Irish Sea to the Pyrennes. Though rebellion flared in Henry's Continental possessions, England enjoyed a period of relative stability during both his reign and that of his son, Richard the Lionheart.

Internal conflict, however, returned to England in the reign of Richard's brother, John. These struggles were not for possession of the throne but for political influence. The great barons wanted to restrict the power of the king and to establish the rule of law. The result was the Magna Carta. If the king was to exceed his authority and flaunt the laws of the land, the charter allowed the barons "to distraut and distress him in every possible way." [1] In the civil war of the thirteenth century this is exactly what the barons were to do.

flout

Any leader who is weak, ineffective or unjust, is likely to face a challenge to his authority. Henry III, to some extent, was all of these. He had failed to fulfil his responsibilities, he had completely mismanaged the economy and he had attempted to rule without the required consultations with his barons. Had he ruled well, there would have been no Battle of Lewes. [2]

Money was in short supply throughout the medieval world and many rents, obligations and debts were paid in kind. Royal grants of land or positions which yielded an income were therefore highly valued. They were also in limited supply. Instead of ensuring that such grants and the income from them were kept circulating within the realm, Henry spent vast sums on military campaigns on the Continent in futile efforts to re-establish his authority over his hereditary lands in France. He also gave away many important posts and a great deal of property in England to his numerous French relations and those of his wife, Eleanor of Provence. The loss of so much money from general circulation, and the excessive influence that the Provencal "foreigners" were able to exert upon Henry, angered

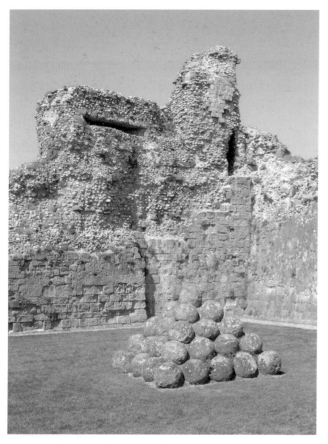

A WWII pillbox built into the ruins of the keep of Pevensey Castle. On the grass below sits a pyramid of catapult stones which may have been used during the many sieges which the castle endured. (By kind permission of the Dircector, Pevensey Castle).

and frustrated the leading figures in England. Though the civil war of the thirteenth century may have worn the gloss of high ideals, in reality it was a conflict driven by jealousy and greed.

Only the great baronial landholders had the strength to challenge the King. His two disastrous military campaigns in France and the virtual bankruptcy of the Crown, forced the barons to act. Ironically, the man who was to emerge as the leader of the English barons in their dispute with King Henry was himself a Frenchman. Simon de Montfort was the younger son of Simon the Crusader who, like so many Anglo-Norman nobles, owned land in both France and England. From the early years of the thirteenth century the holders of property on both sides of the Channel had been persuaded into choosing just one overlord - be it either the King of England or the King of France. Simon the Crusader's eldest son inherited the family lands in France, leaving Simon de Montfort to try and claim the English half of the de Montfort estate.

Though he arrived in England with nothing but ambition, Simon de Montfort managed to secure the title of Earl of Leicester which brought with it the position of Steward of England. In this ceremonial role he waited upon the King at important state functions and he soon became a royal favourite - especially with Eleanor, the King's sister. When Eleanor and Simon married, de Montfort became one of the most powerful man in England.

As his military ventures in France had achieved so little Henry, for once wisely, sought a negotiated peace with King Louis IX. However Henry, urged on by the Pope who had a vested interest in Italian affairs, became embroiled in an attempt to secure the vacant throne of Sicily for his younger son Edmund. Henry promised arms and money for what was, in effect, the Pope's attempt to bring Sicily under papal control. The enterprise was doomed to failure from the outset and with the Pope threatening to excommunicate Henry if he did not fulfil his promises, the King turned to the barons for financial aid. He had undertaken this hopeless venture without consulting the great lords of the realm and they were justifiably determined not to allow Henry to drag England into any more unnecessary conflicts.

Forced into a corner, Henry agreed to a series of reforms which became known as the *Provisions of Oxford* which were promulgated in 1258. The Provisions laid down that the King should rule through a "Council of Fifteen" chosen from the barons and the clergy. The fifteen were required to report to a

The image of Simon de Montfort on the memorial to the Battle of Lewes in the grounds of Lewes Priory. Access to the Priory can be gained from the car park on Mountfield Road, south of Lewes railway station, (TQ 414095). (By kind permission of Lewes Town Council).

parliament which was to be held regularly three times a year. In the Provisions, Henry was bound not to grant land or important positions without the consent of the council, and many of Henry's French relations were driven into exile.

At the beginning of 1261 Henry decided that he had had enough of the restrictions imposed upon him by the hated council. Shutting himself up in the Tower of London, he appointed his own advisors and sent an envoy to the Pope to

seek absolution from the Provisions. In April Henry's envoy returned from Rome with a papal bull that released Henry from his oath. Free at last from the control of the barons Henry left London with a body of mercenary knights hired from France and marched south. He took Rochester and Dover, after which he moved into Sussex securing reluctant promises of allegiance from the men of the Cinque Ports.

In response the barons called a parliament without the

consent of the King. Both sides gathered together their forces and prepared for war. But a few of the leading barons backed down at the last minute. This infuriated de Montfort who then left England to pursue his wife's claims to property in France

The Earl of Leicester returned to England in the spring of 1263 to became the leader of the reformers, after many of the original group that had promoted the Provisions of Oxford had died or defected to the King. Many of the barons were unwilling to push the issue of reform any further. The King had, in fact, undertaken some reforms in local government and because of the strong opposition he had faced it seemed unlikely that he would undertake any more extravagant wars or appoint any more foreigners to important positions in England. It was clear that Henry would not accept any other changes unless forced to do so at the point of a sword and few of the barons were prepared to actually fight the King.

Despite the weakness of their position a renewed effort was made to enforce the Provisions and the barons declared that all who resisted the reforms were enemies of the state. With their supporters under arms, the barons attacked and captured a number of the leading, and least liked, Frenchmen. This prompted uprisings against the established order across the country. In most cases it was the foreign clergy or landholders who were the targets of these attacks.

The King was in London, safe behind the massive walls of the Tower. But he could not remain passively in his capital whilst de Montfort's men took control of the country. Henry's first thought was for the safety of his communications with France and he sent his son Edward to secure Dover. This was accomplished but Henry was penniless and the London merchants were not prepared to forward any kind of loan.

This led Edward to break into the New Temple, (London), which in those days was used as a safe-deposit vault, from where he stole around £1,000 worth of treasure. Though Edward escaped with the loot to Windsor castle, many Londoners had now been pushed into the arms of the barons.

Henry's position was not good and de Montfort hoped to bring the king to terms without having to cross swords with his monarch. Whilst de Montfort's emissaries - in the form of a committee of bishops - negotiated with Henry in London, the Earl's army swept round the capital and marched to the south coast. The men of Dover and the Cinque Ports (see chapter five) readily abandoned their loyalty to the King. With the London mob baying for blood and his communications with the Continent now severed, Henry was trapped.

The King was prepared to accept the demands of the reformers but not so the Queen. Eleanor left the Tower to join Edward at Windsor from where she intended to continue the struggle against the barons. But she was spotted by the mob as she tried to escape and was pelted with mud and stones, being saved from harm by the Mayor of London.

Though Henry and Simon de Montfort finally agreed upon the terms of a settlement, the two parties later decided to take their dispute to arbitration. King Louis IX agreed to be the arbiter and Henry and Simon set off for France shortly after Christmas. Henry arrived safely in Paris but de Montfort was thrown from his horse and broke his leg just twenty miles into his journey. Others had to represent the reformers' cause when the two sides met at the court of the King of France.

Henry's main complaint was that the Oxford Provisions denied him the right to chose his own officials or even his own household. The reformers argued that because of Henry's previous miss-management of state affairs, he could not be allowed unlimited powers. Though the lists of complaints brought by both sides were long and detailed, the principle points of contention were still those of 1258.

Unsurprisingly, Louis, himself an absolute monarch, pronounced in favour of Henry. Louis' decision, enshrined within the *Mise of Amiens*, solved nothing and when Henry returned to England he found his realm divided in conflict. Along the Welsh Marches and as far south as Gloucester, the private armies of the great barons were openly at war with each other.

Though many must have believed in their cause, be they reformers or reactionaries, others saw the conflict as a way to increase their personal power and to avenge earlier wrongs.

On 5 April, Henry's son, the young Prince Edward, attacked Northampton where a number of barons were gathering for a conference which had been called by the Earl of Leicester. Edward captured both the town and the barons before the baronial army, led by de Montfort, could intervene.

When he learnt of the capture of Northampton, de Montfort changed direction and moved upon Rochester. This strategically important town had been occupied and garrisoned on 16 April by two of Henry's supporters, Earl de Warrenne of Lewes and William de Braose of Bramber. The rebel army reached Rochester the day following the fall of Northampton and de Montfort's force surrounded the town. The first attack upon Rochester by the rebels was halted by the defenders setting fire to the southern suburbs of the town. The next day, 18 April, de Montfort drove the garrison from the bailey and into the keep. For the next five days, the baronial army laid siege to the castle but it could not penetrate the great tower.

Edward, meanwhile, had left Northampton with the intention of entering London. When de Montfort was informed of the Royalist threat to the capital he abandoned the siege and returned to London. With the capital held by the rebels Edward crossed the Thames at Kingston and marched round to Rochester where, on 27 April, he relieved the garrison.

In support of Edward's manoeuvres in the south-east Henry, with a large body of infantry, captured the Earl of Gloucester's castle at Tonbridge on 1 May. The two royalist contingents then joined forces and followed in the footsteps of Harold's army 200 years before across the Weald to Senlac Hill. Henry had two reasons for wishing to establish a base in Sussex. Firstly, the great castles at Hastings, Pevensey, Lewes and Arundel were held by the King's adherents. Secondly, Sussex remained the gateway to Normandy where the Queen had already fled to urge the King of France to help support the absolutist cause.

Looking across the Lewes battlefield of 1264 from the point where Simon de Montfort's left wing may have deployed. Access to the battlefield can be reached by footpath from the A275 opposite Offham village, (TQ 395114).

The monks of Battle Abbey wisely welcomed the Royal army but were forced, nevertheless, to hand over a large amount of money for the army's military chest. From Battle the King continued towards the coast, reaching Winchelsea on 3 May. Here Henry appealed for help from the Cinque Ports. He wanted them to send a naval force through the Thames to attack London. The leaders of the Cinque Ports had always supported the baronial cause and they refused to assist the King and they sent their ships out to sea so that they could not be taken by the Royalists. In response Henry took hostages to ensure that the Cinque Ports did not participate actively on behalf of the rebels and he left Winchelsea just two days after his arrival.

This time Henry made for a town held by one of his main allies - Lewes. Marching back through Battle, the Royal army bivouacked at Herstmonceux that night and entered Lewes the following day. Henry, accompanied by his brother Richard, established himself in the Priory of St. Pancras which was just beyond the town walls. Edward joined John de Warenne in the castle.

It was that same day, 6 May, that the baronial army set off

FLETCHING

Blackcap

Mount Harry

OFFHAM HILL

Hamsey Chalk Pits

RIVER OUSE

Simon
De Montfort

Segrave

De Montfort

Gloucester

Edward

Richard

Henry

Landport

LEWES

BRIGHTON

Malling Hill

PRIORY

MOUNT CABURN

THE BROOKS

THE BATTLE OF LEWES 1264

Scale Miles

1/2   0   1   2

1/2   0   1   2   3

Scale Kilometres

from London intent upon tracking down the Royalists and bring them to battle as de Montfort now accepted that the only way to resolve the dispute was by force of arms. The Earl of Leicester seems to have been well-informed and he was aware of Henry's intention of moving to Lewes before the King left Winchelsea.

De Monfort reached the Sussex village of Fletching, covering the forty miles from London in a single day. Like Harold before the Battle of Hastings, the Earl of Leicester had placed his army just a few miles from the encampment of the enemy. His men could now rest and recuperate, knowing that only a short march would place them opposite their opponents. In those days Fletching was still sheltered by the Wealden forest and the village lay adjacent to de Montfort's estate of Sheffield Park [3]. De Montfort must have known the area well and, as an experienced soldier, it is likely that he had the prospective battlefield fixed in his mind long before he marched upon Lewes.

There was now an inexplicable pause in hostilities. For a full week the two armies remained just eight miles apart. On 12 May, de Montfort despatched the Bishop of Chichester to Lewes to negotiate a peace treaty based upon the King's acceptance of the Provisions of Oxford. The offer was rejected. The following day the rebels moved closer to Lewes, but how much closer is not known. [4] It is certain that the army bivouacked in a wood and, as it was to take the Royal army by surprise the next day, it is obvious that the rebels were still far enough away as to be out of visual range from Offham Hill where Henry had posted a lookout. From this "wood by Lewes" [5], de Montfort sent a letter to Henry stating that the barons were not in arms against the King but against his French advisors. Henry's reply was that the barons were rebels and traitors. Battle was now inevitable.

The Earl of Leicester did make good use of some of the time spent at Fletching. He ordered his men to sew white crosses on the fronts and backs of their tunics and hauberks. Not only would this aid identification in the fighting to come, it would also reinforce the belief that their cause was more than just a struggle for power - it was a crusade against government without accountability.

It has been calculated that dawn on Wednesday 14 May 1264 was around 3.00 a.m. [6] Within the hour the baronial army would have been on the move and the first units may have reached the foot of Offham Hill, where the Earl planned to make his stand, by 07.00. This is the time given by Professor Powicke based on the assumption that the rebels had marched all the way from Fletching. As it is known that the barons had moved a little closer to Lewes the day before, it is possible that the first troops may have reached Offham some time earlier. The most likely set of circumstances is that de Montfort achieved his element of surprise by the fact that he had moved to within a few miles of Lewes on the 13th (suggested by David Carpenter as being in the vicinity of Hamsey [7]) allowing him to reach the battlefield soon after sunrise. It is also possible that the rebel army marched through the night and arrived at Mount Harry before dawn. Surprise was essential to de Montfort's plans. The northern facing slopes of the Downs in this area are very steep and, if the King had chosen to defend the ridge, de Montfort's small army would have been severely disadvantaged. De Montfort needed to gain the high ground and his only chance of doing so was if his march to the battlefield was unopposed

Element's of de Montfort's cavalry had scouted around Offham two days earlier where they had encountered a Royalist picket and a minor skirmish had ensued at Combe Hollow. There can be no excuse therefore for the Royalist army being unprepared, yet the rebels quite definitely did achieve some degree of surprise. Only one man of the Royalist picket on Offham Hill was at his post that morning, the others having wandered off. This man was caught asleep and so the barons were able to take up their positions upon Offham Hill without interference. The fact that the sentry was still asleep lends weight to the view that the rebels, or at least some of them, reached Offham whilst it was still dark.

There is some doubt as to the route taken by the rebels up Offham Hill. They must have marched from Fletching along the west bank of the River Ouse. This track passed through a marshy defile, just 500 yards wide, between Offham Hill and the river. If the rebel army was caught in column of march in this defile it

The barbican and gatehouse of Lewes Castle. The castle is on the north side of Lewes High Street, (TQ 414101). (By kind permission of the Sussex Archaeological Society).

the Offham heights from the north.

To reach the top of Offham Hill an ancient sunken track climbs the precipitous northern face of the heights. If the baronial army was to take this track it could do so only in single file. Not only would this mean that, again, the army would be in a highly vulnerable state, it would also take hours for thousands of heavily armed troops to follow one after the other up the track. Another traditional theory is that the rebel troops marched to the west and took one of the paths which run diagonally up Blackcap Hill above Plumpton plain. This idea has been dismissed by at least one historian [8] who has indicated that though this move to the west would enable the climb to be made on a broader front, the increased distance that the troops would have to march would result in no saving of time. It is more likely that many troops climbed directly up Offham Hill but that the rest of the army, some 6,000 or more men, spread out to the west and mounted the hill wherever they could instead of queuing anxiously at the bottom of the track. Some, no doubt, would have gone as far as the pathways up Blackcap Hill. It is possible that this movement towards the west was part of de Montfort's planned deployment, with those troops that were to form the right wing being the ones that climbed the heights near Blackcap.

Other evidence indicates that the rebel army, which might have been stationed at Hamsey throughout the 13th, chose the more circuitous route via Blackcap and Mount Harry to surprise and confuse the Royalist lookouts on Offham Hill. It is stated in the *Gilson fragment* that "the army of the barons came to Boxholte, which is two leagues distant from Lewes".[9] Boxholte has been placed some 500 yards south-west of Blackcap from where there is an easy ascent to the top of the Downs.[10]

Henry's neglect in failing to post an adequate picket with his enemy so close may seem extraordinary. Yet pitched battles were rare events in medieval England and Henry probably believed that he was in little danger. Lewes Castle was a formidable defensive structure with its two mottes and strong bailey. The town itself was walled and beyond its gates lay an army that was far stronger than de Montfort's band of rebels. Though de

would have had no room to manoeuvre or be able to find sufficient ground to form line of battle. It would be destroyed piecemeal by the superior numbers of the enemy. To the east of Lewes are the steep sides of Malling Hill and to the south and north of the town is the marshy flood plain of the Ouse. The relatively easy southern facing slopes of Offham Hill and the adjoining Mount Harry to the north-west of the town offered de Monfort the only suitable field for battle. As he dare not attempt to force the passage of the Offham defile de Montfort had to scale

Montfort had marched quickly from London he had shown no aggressive signs since halting at Fletching, almost as if he hoped that the threat of armed revolt would induce Henry to seek a compromise with the barons. It is likely that Henry hoped that he would not have to fight a battle at Lewes and even if de Montfort did try to attack the town his only practicable route was along the west bank of the Ouse. From the top of Offham Hill, with its commanding views across the Ouse valley, a single sentry would suffice to warn of any approach from the north.

It was not, therefore, in a lack of adequate lookouts that Henry showed his weakness as a general, rather it was in allowing de Montfort to choose the time and place of battle. A stronger man, a Harold Godwin or a William of Normandy, would have marched to face the rebels and forced them to fight on his terms.

But the King simply sat (or slept) and waited whilst the Earl of Leicester's men formed line of battle upon the gentle southern slopes of Offham Hill. De Montfort arranged his force in the now traditional three divisions or "wards", but to this he added a reserve ward. The addition of this reserve is considered by historians to have been an innovation in medieval warfare and its introduction into the battle at a crucial stage in the fight was to prove instrumental in securing an unexpected victory for the small rebel army.

Initially, the baronial army took up a position just below the former site of the Racecourse grandstand, running north-westwards to the top of what is now the disused chalk pit overlooking the River Ouse. Spanning a distance of 1,000 yards, and taking into account the small force of cavalry and the gaps between the divisions, each ward would possibly have assembled five ranks deep. Of the three wards, the right wing, composed of de Montfort's best troops, was under the command of his two sons, Henry and Guy. The centre ward was led by Gilbert de Clare, the Earl of Gloucester, and the left, the weakest of the three, was commanded by Nicholas de Segrave. There is no record of who led the reserve and it is probable that this body remained under de Montfort's personal control. The Earl of

The motte and remains of the keep of Lewes Castle. (By kind permission of Sussex Archaeological Society).

Leicester was conveyed to the battlefield in a coach, or cart, as his leg, which had been broken on his abortive trip to Paris, had not fully healed.

De Montfort's army has been estimated at around 5,000 to 6,000 men of which only 500 were mounted. Of this force the left ward, (under de Segrave), was made up of volunteers gathered by de Montfort at London. The volunteers owed allegiance to nothing but the cause, whereas the rest of the rebel army was principally composed of vassals of the barons that supported de Montfort. These men, whose lives, property and prosperity were bound up with the fortunes of their baronial overlords, had more at stake than just ideals. They had natural command structures and were well-armed; many would have been armed retainers - trained, disciplined and professional soldiers.

The knights of both armies, including the great barons,

would have worn a chain-mail hauberk little different from that used by the Normans in 1066. The hauberk had long sleeves and a hood, or "coif". An elaborate helm, which completely enclosed the head, was worn over the coif. The legs were also protected by chain mail in the form of a stocking (called a chausse). Over the hauberk would be a surcoat of cotton or silk which reached down to the ankles. Usually decorated with heraldic devices, at Lewes the baronial army replaced or covered their surcoats with the white crosses prepared at Fletching. Whilst the fully armoured knight was still in the future, by the time of the Battle of Lewes some of the wealthy knights were already adding plate armour reinforcement to the knees, elbows and shins.

The knights were trained and experienced soldiers. Taught to ride and fight from their youth, many of the knights had campaigned in France and fought against the Welsh. When not actually at war, the knights practised their art at the great tournaments held throughout the land and even on the Continent. Their weapons were the lance and sword added to which was the shield, emblazoned with the knights' coat-of-arms. Their mounts were specially-bred and highly expensive war horses.

The mounted retainers might have possessed no more than a helmet and a leather jerkin or padded doublet. This was also as much protection as the foot soldiers would have worn. Usually armed with pikes, swords and daggers, the infantry also carried longbows. The bow was to become the pre-eminent battlefield weapon a hundred years later in the great battles of Crecy and Agincourt where they were used en masse and in controlled volleys. Such tactics had not been developed by the middle of the twelfth century despite the known success achieved by William's archers at Hastings.

After they had assembled into their allotted positions de Montfort ordered his men to kneel in prayer. It is said that they flung themselves onto the grass with their arms outstretched to form the shape of a cross.

Much ink has been used to debate the exact location of the battle. Interesting though such scholarly work may be, it is difficult to accept that the battle was fought in any one particular place. Though it seems positive that the baronial forces stood in battle array upon the Offham heights it is far from certain that they remained stationary when the king's army marched into view. As the skeletons of the unfortunate victims of the slaughter have been found in considerable quantities as far apart as the site of the Offham chalk pits and Lewes Prison, it appears evident that the battle raged the length and breadth of the southern facing slopes of the Downs from Offham Hill to the walls of the town.

Offham Hill is clearly visible from the keep of Lewes Castle one and a half miles to the south-east, and it is hard to believe that the movement of large bodies of troops on the hill could have gone unnoticed for long. It is said that the Royalist's attack began at 09.45 and we have estimated that the latest time the first of the rebel troops climbed Offham Hill was at around 07.00. It cannot have taken almost three hours for Henry's troops to arm themselves and move the mile or so from the limits of the old town to the start line. So it must be deduced that, as far as was possible, de Montfort's troops formed up on the north facing slopes of the hill and only marched over the crest and into the (presumably) pre-arranged positions on the southern-facing slopes when they were assembled in battle array.

The Royalist cavalry, numbering some 3,000 men in total, was watering its horses along the banks of the Ouse when the first alarm was given. This body is usually stated as being composed of mounted knights. Yet there were only 1,000 to 2,000 knights in the entire country and not all of them were present nor were they all Royal supporters. At least half of Edward's cavalry must have included paid retainers and other men-at-arms.

The pages and grooms rushed their masters' horses back to the town. The mounts were saddled, the knights pulled on their hauberks, grabbed shields, swords and helmets and trotted out to Landport Bottom. It is stated by some authorities that Edward attacked the rebels without waiting for the rest of the Royal army and it is assumed, though not recorded, that Edward passed a message on to his father that he was going to attack without delay. Other sources indicate that the Royal army was drawn up correctly before the engagement, with the three wards alongside each other in the traditional manner. Edward was a natural warrior and already experienced in warfare and it is extremely unlikely that he would have charged into the baronial forces unsupported. Edward's force, being mounted and therefore highly mobile, probably left the other two wards behind as it advanced up the hill.

Edward's division described as "the flower of the army"[11] included many of the most prominent Royal barons. John de Warenne, William de Valance, Hugh Bigod, Roger Mortimore and the Marcher lords were all numbered amongst the heir to the throne's division and, when formed in line of battle, would have occupied the Royalist right wing. Leaving the rest of the army to catch up with him, Edward led his magnificent force of heavily armoured knights into battle. Usually in medieval battles the two forces formed up in battle array opposite each other, with care being taken to ensure that the armies did not overlap before battle was joined. By rushing up the hill before the rest of the Royal army was in place, Edward displayed not just his bravery but also his impetuosity. It would cost his father the battle.

Though the slope of the hill from Landport is not severe the horses, with their iron-clad riders, would only have moved up the incline at a walk. Before them, on the left of the baronial army, stood Nicholas de Segrave's ill-equipped band of Londoners. Ahead of the Londoners was a body of high-ranking troops, probably mounted knights which included John Gifford. When Edward's men were just a short distance from de Segrave's line, the horses would have been spurred into a trot. As the two forces closed to within a few yards of each other the infantry would have fired their bows or released their slings as the cavalry urged their mounts into a full gallop.

The Royalists crashed into de Segrave's ward, scattering the Londoners in all directions and John Gifford, in his determination to be the first man to strike a blow for the barons, was captured. With their formation broken the infantrymen

The helm-shaped monument to the Battle of Lewes in the grounds of Lewes Priory. (By kind permission of Lewes Town Council).

stood no chance against the knights. It seems certain that this clash occurred immediately above the chalkpits as large numbers of skeletons have been discovered during the quarrying of the chalk. The bodies were buried in small pits containing from six to nine bodies in each. The knights pursued the broken infantrymen along the northern face of the Downs towards Blackcap (for bodies have also been recovered from there) whilst others chased the fleeing Londoners down the steep northern slopes of Offham Hill. The pursuit continued along the banks of the Ouse, into which river as many as sixty of the rebels may have drowned.

It is said that the pursuit lasted for four miles and Edward, again showing his exuberance, allowed his horsemen to get completely out of control. He had utterly destroyed de Montfort's left division. It was never able to reform and some of the rebels did not stop running until they reached London. But the knights had themselves incurred casualties, with many horses, no doubt, stumbling and falling down the precipitous decline from Offham Hill. Nevertheless, if Edward would have been able to reform his men and return to the battlefield at this stage of the engagement his achievement would have been considerable. However, this did not happen. By the time Edward had gathered his scattered horsemen and marched them back up Offham Hill the battle was all but over. De Montfort lost his weakest infantry division. Henry had lost his elite force of cavalry. The odds, which had been decidedly in favour of the Royalists before battle was joined, were now even.

De Montfort and the remainder of the baronial army did not know that the battle was developing to their advantage. They had seen a quarter of their force flee from the battlefield and they knew that it would only be a matter of time before the Royalist cavalry returned. The rest of the Royal army, possibly 6,000 strong, was marching across Landport Bottom towards them. It would not have been surprising if the rebel army had disintegrated. This must have been an anxious time for the Earl of Leicester. But de Montfort and his men stood their ground.

Henry, also, must have been a worried man. Offham Hill cannot be seen from the Priory nor from the paths leading out of Lewes and it is likely that he had not seen Edward's charge. When he arrived at Landport Bottom and looked up the hill he would have seen de Montfort's army posted on the heights and not a sign of his elite cavalry force!

The King, in conventional fashion, had divided his force into three wards. Edward had disappeared with the right-hand ward leaving Henry with his own central ward and the left ward under the command of Edward's brother Richard, Duke of Cornwall. [12] The ground up which the Royalists had to climb starts from where the present-day prison stands with a slope of 1 in 9. [13]

At 600 yards from the prison the incline decreases to just 1 in 30 but the ground slips away to the east to form a shallow hollow. Richard of Cornwall's men would have marched along the higher ground, possibly with some of them moving along the sides of the hollow. Henry's division would have advanced up the hollow where the gradient increases to 1 in 8. Even on level ground it is not easy for a large body of men to maintain formation - up the undulating slopes of Offham Hill it would have been very difficult.

It would seem that the two Royalist divisions attacked simultaneously. Richard's force, opposed by the strongest division - the right ward - of the rebel army, met with a hail of arrows and sling-stones. This, the weakest of the Royalist divisions, gave way, leaving Henry's men isolated on the hill. It was at this moment that the Earl of Leicester threw his reserve into the action. These fresh troops joined the rest of de Montfort's force, including the cavalry, and drove Henry back down the slope. It is equally possible that de Montfort did not wait to be attacked but instead charged downhill upon the Royalists as soon as they climbed into view.

At the bottom of the hill, somewhere near the prison, Henry rallied his men and made a stand. Here was the scene of the greatest slaughter, for three large pits were unearthed when the turnpike road from Brighton was being improved in 1810. Each pit contained around 500 skeletons and it took many days to remove them all. Such a concentration of bodies has led many to speculate that the main action of the battle took place at this point rather than on the slopes of Offham Hill. Indeed, it may well be that de Montfort attacked the centre and left Royalist wards as they were forming up outside the walls of the town. Yet casualties occur on a greater scale in battle when one side has broken and turned its back upon the enemy. It may well be that it was here that the retreating Royalists were caught by the pursuing rebels.

Henry fought bravely. Two horses were killed under him and he was wounded and bruised. He and his remaining followers escaped back into the Priory whilst Richard of Cornwall hid in a windmill on the southern part of the battlefield where he was surrounded by his jeering enemies. One historian has suggested that this was a water-mill on the marshes by the Ouse. [14] The mill proved an inadequate refuge and Richard was driven out and into the arms of his enemies.

The fighting spread into the town and beyond. Why the Royalists did not escape into the safety of the Castle - the most obvious course of action - remains a mystery. The most likely explanation is that the opposing forces had become so inextricably intermixed that the garrison dare not open the gates for fear of letting the rebels into the Castle.

It was at this stage of the battle that Edward re-appeared on the battlefield. The time that Royalist cavalry returned has been calculated at approximately 14.30 hours. This means that the knights had been absent from the field for at least four hours. Edward's men and their mounts were so exhausted after chasing around for so long that they could barely walk. He found the battlefield deserted apart from the dead and wounded and the captured Royalists that were in the hands of the rebels. Possibly still unaware of the course of the battle Edward saw the coach with de Montfort's banner flying from it on top of the hill. The Prince immediately attacked the coach and slaughtered everyone inside. Unfortunately these were Royalist prisoners who were unable to make their identities known before they were killed. It is possible that the placing of de Montfort's carriage on the top of the hill had been a deliberate ploy to mask the Earl's true whereabouts.

In and around Lewes the battle still raged and de Warenne's banner still flew from the Castle keep. All might not be lost. Edward rode down to Lewes still hoping, no doubt, to turn the tide of battle once again in his favour. It seems that he did not fall upon the rear of the rebels but instead he skirted Lewes to combine forces with the Royalists who were still defending the town. He cut his way through to the priory and joined the King.

The fighting continued in the town, with the Royalists and the rebels still hacking away at each other. The town was in flames, caused by fire-arrows shot from the battlements of the Castle, and the streets were littered with the dead and the dying. Beyond the town the fugitives from the bloodshed tried to escape over the bridge and across the fords.[15] Many of the heavily-clad warriors fell to their deaths in the river and others met a similar fate in the marshes (The Brooks) to the south of the town.

Another critical moment in the battle occurred when de Warenne, along with 300 to 400 of Edward's men, gave up the struggle and rode away.

The Priory now came under direct assault from the rebels. Edward gathered his remaining troops in preparation for a counter-attack when de Montfort sent a message into the priory proposing an armistice. The offer was accepted and the Battle of Lewes came to an end.

Casualties have been estimated at more than 3,000 because in addition to the burial pits unearthed in 1810, more bodies were found in 1846 when the railway was laid across the grounds of the St. Pancras Priory. This means that, as probably only 16,000 men took part in the battle, around twenty per cent of all the combatants were either killed or seriously wounded. We know that few knights were killed so most of the casualties came from the foot soldiers. Some of the Royalists escaped to Pevensey Castle and some fled to France to join the Queen. Others were not so fortunate. It is said that a group of fugitives were cornered and butchered at a point near East Hoathly some six and a half miles to the north-east of Lewes. The place is still known as Terrible Down.[16]

Simon de Montfort had won the battle, now he had to win the peace. Throughout the night and the following day the negotiations to establish a limited form of democratic government began. The battle had destroyed Henry's will to resist and he formally surrendered his sword to de Clare. He allowed himself to be taken prisoner by the barons before negotiations began, even though the Priory was held by a large body of Royal troops and Edward and Richard's son Henry had managed to establish themselves in the Castle which was still well-defended. During the following day, Thursday 15th, the friars from the Priory carried messages between the barons in the Priory and the Royalists in the Castle. From the moment of Henry's capture, however, it was obvious that the negotiations could only have one conclusion - the restoration of the Provisions of Oxford. On the Friday Edward and the young Henry gave themselves up as hostages in place of the King and his brother Richard. By Saturday Henry had succumbed and a letter, in the King's name, went out to his supporters ordering them to hand over their castles to the rebels.

De Montfort's success at Lewes was seen as "miraculous" [17] but it was not the kind of decisive victory won by William at Hastings. Henry had not died where he fought and the Royalist party remained strong. Many northern earls and the powerful Marcher barons had escaped and were certain to oppose de Montfort's authority. Even in Sussex, which had seen enough death and destruction, the Royalists continued to resist. After the Battle of Lewes the Constable of Pevensey had been ordered to hand over the Castle - to which some of the Royalists had fled after the battle - to the barons. He refused and, not for the first or last time, the Castle found itself under siege.

De Montfort seems to have genuinely wished to establish a sound system of elected government based on an agreed, written constitution. It was, after all, the only way that he could justify taking up arms against his King. But so many of the country's leading men had fought for the King and they would never agree to the constitutional reforms de Montfort wished. Too much blood had been shed for there to be any possibility of peace. The conflict was no longer about ideals - if indeed it ever had been - it had now become personal.

The settlement after the battle was termed "The Mise of Lewes". Under the terms of the settlement, Henry was to be advised by a council of nine chosen by three electors, the principle member of which was the Earl of Leicester. In reality the arrangement was little more than a dictatorship controlled by de Montfort. This, the very opposite from the aims of the barons who had supported constitutional change, alienated many of de Montfort's followers.

Though de Montfort did call a parliament, in which representatives of the shires and boroughs as well as the barons and the clergy sat together and discussed the business of the country's affairs, his reactionary enemies were too strong. The King remained a virtual prisoner, often being compelled to follow de Montfort in the earl's entourage. Edward was under guard at all times and Richard of Cornwall was kept in luxurious captivity at Kenilworth Castle. By keeping the principle royal males under his close control, de Montfort must have hoped to deter the Royalists from direct aggression. It had the opposite effect.

Queen Eleanor, who was still in France, tried to raise an army for the invasion of England and throughout the summer of 1265 de Montfort's troops were stationed along the south-east coast. As the months passed by de Montfort's support declined. His assumption of an almost regal state and the seizure of land and property to add to the de Montfort estates drove many more into the Royalist camp. Finally, his failure to adequately reward the Earl of Gloucester for his part in the great victory at Lewes forced de Montfort's most powerful ally to turn against him.

Simon de Montfort ruled England for less than fifteen months. Towards the end of July 1265, Edward slipped away from his guards and joined Gilbert de Clare. Together, the Earl of Gloucester and the Prince marched upon de Montfort at Evesham. Once again de Montfort faced a Royalist force which greatly exceeded his own. This time, though, the odds were too great even for the Earl of Leicester. De Montfort was killed and his body mutilated by his angry enemies.

Henry was succeeded by his son Edward. Though a strong and successful ruler, Edward I learnt from the conflict with the barons. He maintained regular parliaments and worked through them instead of against them. Though this was forced upon him through financial necessity, it firmly established the principle of rule by democracy which had first occurred in England after Simon de Montfort's great victory at Lewes.

In 1965 a monument was erected at Simon de Montfort's grave at Evesham. It was unveiled by the Speaker of the House of Commons to acknowledge de Montfort's legacy - the English Parliament.

5
Defence of the Realm
The wars at sea

It has long been an axiom that, as an island, Britain's best defence was to attack the enemy at sea and for many centuries the warships and sailors from the Cinque Ports of Sussex formed part of England's coastal defence. The Cinque Ports were a maritime confederacy whose privileges and duties were legally defined by a Royal Charter of 1278. In return for the defence of the coast against sea-borne incursions and the provision of fifty-seven armed ships and crews for fifteen days each year for the Royal fleet, the confederation was granted certain rights and privileges. These included exemption from many taxes, the rights of wreckage (an important, if irregular, source of income) and Honours at Court. If the ships were required for longer than the fifteen days the king had to pay for their services.

The original five ports were Hastings, Romney, Hythe, Dover and Sandwich with Winchelsea and Rye as attached members of Hastings. The full title of the confederation was the Cinque Ports and Two Ancient Towns. At various times throughout the Middle Ages other towns and ports, from as far as Brightlingsea in Essex to Seaford in Sussex (and including Pevensey and Bulverhythe), were affiliated with the confederation, forming one of the most important naval forces in England. At the height of its power and influence the Confederation numbered no less than forty-two towns and villages. [1]

The ports had been active as a confederation long before their position was legally established. It is known that the Cinque Ports' fleet sailed up the eastern coast in support of King Harold's march to York to face Hardrada's Vikings in 1066. Unfortunately for Harold these vessels were still in the north when William sailed from Normandy and the Conqueror found the coast undefended. [2] Ironically, it was the loss of Normandy by King John in 1204 which thrust the south coast and the Cinque Ports into the front line defence of England.

Their first recorded large-scale battle occurred early in 1213 when the Cinque Ports' fleet attacked Dieppe and destroyed French ships which had been assembling in the Seine estuary in preparation for an attack upon England. In May of the same year the Cinque Ports' ships formed part of an English naval force which defeated the French at the Battle of Damme where, it was claimed, the Portsmen captured 200 enemy vessels.

In 1216 Rye and Winchelsea opened their gates to the Dauphin of France in his unsuccessful bid to wrest the English throne from the hated King John. The French also occupied Chichester Castle. The following year the Castle was re-captured and the Cinque Ports fleet, having been bribed to change sides, defeated the French navy in a battle off Sandwich. So that Chichester Castle could never be used again by the French it was pulled down in 1225.

In 1242 the Cinque Ports were granted permission to ravage the French coast but it was during the Hundred Years War (1337-1453) that the men and the ships of the Cinque Ports were most frequently in action. This conflict was a continuation of the confusion that arose after William the Conqueror divided his Anglo-Norman empire between his sons. From that moment on, the leading men in England and France were locked in seemingly endless disputes over the rights to property on both sides of the Channel. Often this took the form of legal debate but sometimes the arguments were decided by the force of arms. So when Phillip VI seized Gascony in 1337 the English king - Edward III- went to war to regain his Gascon possessions and to assert his own claim to the throne of France.

The first battle of the Hundred Years War was at sea. Edward, with a massive fleet of ships, including a large contingent from the Cinque Ports, achieved a great victory off Sluys. French losses

Winchelsea's Pipewell Gate which is situated to the north-west of the town, (TQ 905174).

The Strand Gate at the eastern corner of Winchelsea town, overlooking the River Brede.

were claimed to have reached 25,000 men. The significance of this victory, and of another success by the Cinque Ports' fleet at Les Espagnols-sur-Mer off Winchelsea in 1350, was that Edward's army was able to cross the Channel and most of the fighting of the Hundred Years War took place in France.[3]

Inevitably the French fleet felt obliged to retaliate and the Sussex coast, particularly the Cinque Ports, came under attack. Winchelsea was first assaulted in 1337 when around a hundred houses were burnt to the ground. Rye suffered a similar raid in 1339 when fifty of its houses were destroyed. Twenty years later, on Sunday 15 March 1359, some 3,000 Frenchmen landed whilst the townspeople were in Winchelsea's Church of St. Giles celebrating Mass. The French broke into the church killing and raping. Forty of the inhabitants were murdered before help came. In the ensuing conflict some 400 English were drowned in the harbour. When the French sailed away they took with them thirteen well-laden ships. [4]

Exactly one year later, on 15 March 1360, Rye and Winchelsea suffered another raid, with both ports and the surrounding countryside being ravaged and burnt. A retaliatory raid was made by the Cinque Ports' fleet a few months later.

The largest French raid came in 1377. Rye was overrun and all the wooden buildings in the town were burnt. Rye's small Castle, the Badding's Tower, which had been built in the time of Henry III, proved incapable of defending the town against such attacks and it was clear that Rye would have to be properly fortified. With the help of Royal grants a stone wall was subsequently erected around the town with impressive strong-points in the form of the Land Gate and the Strand Gate. Baddings Tower was sold to a private individual, John de Ypres, in 1430 and has been known as the Ypres Tower ever since.

The French raiders then moved against Winchelsea. But the Abbot of Battle, having learnt of the French incursion, armed his men and sent them to help man the town's defences. The raiders were driven off. Winchelsea's defences were formed when the new town was built on it's present site at the end of the 13th century. It's walls were partly wood and earth, with stone only being used at key locations. The whole of the eastern side was surrounded by a wide ditch.

Undeterred by their repulse at Winchelsea, the French continued along the coast, ransacking Hastings and destroying its churches. Hastings was no longer the major port in the region. Hastings heads the list of the Cinque Ports and at its height in the twelfth century it contributed twenty ships to the king's fleet. By the early thirteenth century Hastings' contribution to the confederation was no more than half-a-dozen vessels. [5] Hastings castle had also declined in importance and as early as 1339 the town and the castle had been ransacked by one of the first raids of the Hundred Years War.

The French attackers continued westwards and reached Rottingdean where the monks from the St. Pancras Priory at Lewes helped to fight off the raiders. Ecclesiastical establishments of the Middle Ages played an important part in local defence, especially as places of refuge. The great gatehouses of places like Battle Abbey and Michelham Priory, as well as the moats dug around churches, such as that at West Tarring, were genuine defensive structures. [6]

In retaliation for the raid of 1377 the men of Rye and Winchelsea attacked the French coast the following year. They captured all the wealthy people that could be held to ransom and they recovered the church bells of the two towns which had been taken by the French the previous year.

The French attacked the Sussex coast again in 1380. Led by Admiral Jean de Vienne, the Cinque Ports of Rye, Winchelsea and Hastings were once more the main targets of the raiders. The final French raid of the Hundred Years War was against Rye in 1448.

The repeated French attacks prompted a number of important landowners living close to the coast to build castles.

Amongst those was Bishop William Rede who sought a

Rye's Land Gate which is in the north-eastern corner of the old town at the junction of Landgate and Tower Street, (TQ 922202).

license to crenellate his house at Amberley after the raid of 1377. Though Amberley is more than six miles from the sea, it is less than a mile from the Arun which French ships could easily navigate. With curtain walls reaching forty feet in height the castle was protected by a moat along its southern face and the extensive marsh land of the Wild Brooks to the north and west. Its most impressive feature was its twin-towered gatehouse, built with a drawbridge and portcullis. Amberley Castle was attacked only once, in 1643 during the Civil War, when it was captured without a struggle by the Parliamentarians.

Around the same time that Amberley Castle was being fortified, Roger de Ashburnham also received permission to strengthen his manor house at Scotney. Until the nineteenth century boundary changes Scotney was in Sussex, but is now in Kent. A few years later, on 21 October 1385, [7] Sir Edward Dalngrigge received a licence to crenellate his property at Bodiam. Like Amberley, Bodiam Castle is near to one of Sussex's major rivers. In this instance the Castle overlooks the River

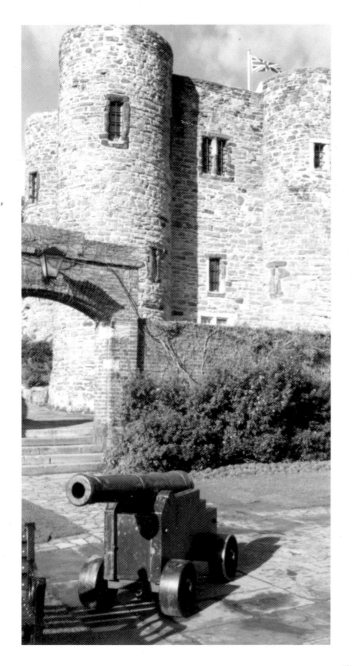

Rother, close to an ancient harbour which had been in use since Roman times.

Bodiam, one of the most picturesque castles in England, was built within a huge rectangular moat, some eight feet deep, which measures 542 feet by 340 feet. Rising to forty-one feet above the level of the water, the short curtain walls are flanked by four circular drum towers at each corner of this virtually square building. Mid-way along each of the southern, eastern and western walls is a rectangular tower and the northern wall boasts an impressive gatehouse. The towers stand twenty feet higher than the walls. Bodiam is classified as a courtyard castle which means that the internal buildings are set around a central courtyard.

The towers of the gatehouse flank the entrance which was built with three portcullises and a drawbridge which led to a barbican gate. A second drawbridge led to a small octagonal island which was reached by a bridge from the western side of the moat. It is also known that the castle was armed with a 15-inch "bombard", one of the earliest types of artillery piece, as one of these guns was found in the moat. This weapon is now on display in the Royal Artillery Museum at Woolwich. With such defences, the castle would have been virtually unassailable, yet the only occasion that it was attacked - during the Civil War - it appears to have been given up without a fight. Bodiam was also besieged in 1483 but nothing is known about the event. [8]

Herstmonceux Castle was built in the penultimate decade of the Hundred Years War by Roger de Fiennes who made his fortune fighting, and plundering, the French. Though the castle is not near a navigable river it does command the exposed Pevensey Levels. Despite its impressive double-parapeted gatehouse and water-filled moat, Herstmonceux is considered to be more a fortified manor house than a true castle.

During this period of unrest Pevensey castle was garrisoned

The Ypres Tower at the south-eastern corner of Rye old town, adjacent to the church. In the foreground is a cannon in the Gun Garden, (TQ 922202).

The front view of Bodium Castle, showing the main gate and barbican. Bodium Castle is signposted from the B2244 to the north-east of Robertsbridge, (TQ 785256). (By kind permission of Mr. D.F. Mace, and the National Trust).

with around twenty or thirty men, usually consisting of ten men-at-arms, twenty bowmen and a watchman. However, in 1372 the Castle passed into the hands of John of Gaunt, the Duke of Lancaster, and he refused to defend the Castle against the French raids. His failure to provide troops to garrison the Castle during the 1377 raid (claiming that if the Castle was damaged he could afford to re-build it!) made the Duke an unpopular figure. During the Peasant's Revolt four years later the locals had their revenge and a mob broke into the Castle and burnt the court rolls used for assessing the Poll Tax. A similar attack was made at this time upon Lewes Castle.

In 1394 John of Gaunt went to Ireland and he entrusted the Constableship of Pevensey Castle to Sir John Pelham. When, five years later, John of Gaunt's son Henry Bolingbroke, clashed with Richard II, Pelham remained loyal to the Gaunt family and Pevensey Castle found itself under siege for the final time in its history. On this occasion the Castle, held by Pelham's wife Joan, was not taken and after Bolingbroke was crowned Henry IV, Pelham received the Castle and Honour of Pevensey as his reward.

With the ending of the Hundred Years War, the military importance of the Cinque Ports faded. Their decline was due in part to the growth of the Royal Navy but also to the silting up of the harbours. Only Dover, with aid from the state, has managed to keep its harbour open. The Cinque Ports were called to defend the realm just one more time when England faced its severest test since 1066. This time, though, it was not from France that the

The southern face of Bodium Castle. (By kind permission of Mr. D.F. Mace and the National Trust).

One of the two "demi-culverns" that were placed in a battery within the outer bailey of Pevensey Castle at the time of the Spanish Armada. The gun is on display inside Pevensey Castle, (TQ 664048). (by kind permission of the Director of Pevensey Castle)

would-be invaders came, but from Spain.

Religion, which has so often whipped up the storm of international conflict, was the wind behind the sails of the magnificent armada of war ships that departed Spain in 1588 intent upon the subjugation of liberal England. Catholic Spain, then the most powerful nation in Europe, numbered the Netherlands (present day Belgium and Holland) amongst its possessions. The growing Protestant movement in the Low Countries worried the severely orthodox Spanish monarch, Philip II, and he decided to end the advance of the heretics and enforce strict Catholicism upon his wayward Dutch and Flemish subjects.

A strong force of mercenaries from Spain's Italian provinces, led by the Duke of Alva, was despatched to the Netherlands in the summer of 1567. Alva arrested the province's leading figures and instigated a reign of inquisitorial terror against the defenceless Protestants. Many fled the Inquisition by crossing the North Sea. The Low Countries had long been England's commercial inlet into Europe and the Flemish weavers and Dutch merchants received a friendly welcome from their old trading partners in Protestant England.

Tension between England and Spain was heightened the following year with the capture of an English fleet of ships in the Caribbean by the Spaniards, and by the retention of the cargo from a Spanish convoy that had sought shelter in the ports along the south coast. That cargo was gold bullion which had been destined to pay the troops occupying the Netherlands. Firstly Spain and then England responded by placing embargoes on each other's trade with the Low Countries.

Relationships between the two countries deteriorated even further when Mary Queen of Scots attempted to seize the English throne with the assistance of the Spaniards. Mary's Catholic supporters captured Hartlepool to allow Alva's men a secure disembarkation but the Spaniards lacked the naval strength to ensure a safe crossing of the North Sea and the rebellion was quickly quashed.

By contrast, northern Europe continued to experience great civil unrest amidst Reformation and Counter-Reformation. It was, therefore, in England's settled shires that industry could flourish in peace. In Sussex the Wealden forests glowed with the fires of the gun foundries. Firstly for the ships of the Royal Navy and then for the forts and castles of the shores, the cannon of Sussex armed the nation. And none too soon. For the dare-devil actions of English privateers on the Spanish Main and open support for the Dutch rebels had enraged Philip and he would tolerate England's interference no longer. 9

Philip planned to crush England with overwhelming force. An armada of transport vessels and warships, led by Medina Sidonia, would sail into the Channel and drive the Royal Navy from its home waters. At the same time the army in the Netherlands, now under the command of the Duke of Parma, would cross the North Sea on flat-bottomed barges taken from the waterways of Flanders.

Elizabeth, and her advisers, were well aware of Philip's preparations and whilst all effort was to be concentrated upon stopping the Spaniards at sea, consideration was also given to the defence of the coast.

Firstly, a chain of fire beacons was established along the entire southern and eastern coastlines. They were formed in pairs. Lighting one beacon was to indicate a small raid which might be repelled by local men; lighting both beacons meant that a full-scale attack was imminent. In Sussex these were located at West Wittering, Bracklesham, Selsey, Sidlesham, The Trundle, Pagham, Felpham, Littlehampton, East Preston, Kingston, Ferring, Goring, Worthing (Heene Mill), East Worthing, Lancing, Aldrington, Brighton, Rottingdean, Seaford (Bishopstone), Wilmington, Willingdon, Beachy Head, Cross-in-Hand, Burwash, Cooden Down and Fairlight. 10 From the coast the alarm could be passed all the way to London with beacons on Highdown Hill, Chanctonbury Ring, Ditchling Beacon, Firle Beacon and Crowborough Beacon transmitting signals to the North Downs and from there to the capital. The maintenance of the beacons, which were pitch-filled iron baskets on top of wooden poles, was

the responsibility of the community and five householders were to oversee each pair. These householders had to ensure that at least two of them were home at all times and no-one living on or near the coast was allowed to move home without permission. The beacon system was supplemented by a relay of post-horses which were held in readiness along the coast. 11

Secondly, batteries were to be built or restored and armed with cannon, especially along the flat, open beaches between Brighton and Selsey. Brighton, a frequent target of raids from the sea, already possessed a gun garden and blockhouse. Situated on what was once a low cliff between the present-day Black Lion Street and Ship Street, the gun garden fronted the sea with the circular blockhouse standing to a height of eighteen feet placed behind it. Initially sixteen guns were housed in the garden and blockhouse but by the time of the Armada this had been reduced to just six. Trenches already existed at Whitehawk Hill and others were planned for Saltdean. Further to the east, Newhaven, East Blatchington and Cuckmere Haven were to be provided with more substantial earthworks and Birling Gap was to be "rammed up". Alfriston, Eastbourne and Hastings were all to receive defensive works or ordnance. A two-gun battery was formed inside the outer bailey of Pevensey Castle, and Camber Castle was kept in good condition and was well-armed. At Rye, still an important port, the Gun Garden was furnished with artillery as was the Land Gate and the Strand Gate. 12

At Shoreham a small defensive work for three guns was raised on the east bank estuary of the Adur. Further west, at Littlehampton (then still known as Arundel

A modern reproduction of a fire beacon. This example is at West Wittering Beach, (SZ 768984).

A French cannon of a type used in the Battle of Beachy Head. It fired a 5-6 pound ball and was located on the upper decks of the ships. It is on display at the entrance to the Eastbourne Redoubt. (By kind permission of the Sussex Combined Services Museum, Eastbourne).

Ambereley Castle's main gate. The Castle is situated off the B2139, (TQ 031132).

Haven) it is possible that a fort was erected on the east bank of the Arun to house four medium calibre cannon. At Kingston (near East Preston), Goring, Worthing and Lancing defensive trenches were dug but they do not appear to have been armed with artillery. Pagham Harbour was particularly well defended with a battery at, or near, East Beach (East Norton) to accommodate three guns, with another three pieces mounted on the eastern arm of the harbour entrance. The height of the former Norman ringwork at Church Norton overlooking the southern edge of the harbour was raised and used as a lookout post. [13]

Responsibility for the defence of the coast from Kent to Dorset was placed in the hands of 'Black' Sir John Norris with the defence of Sussex delegated to Lord Howard of Effingham - the Lord Admiral of England - who held the title of Lord Lieutenant of Sussex and Surrey. He was assisted by the Queen's cousin Lord Brockhurst. Lewes, situated in the middle of the county, was selected as the military headquarters and Brockhurst moved into the town. The house where he stayed still stands and is now "Shelley's Hotel" in the High Street. The county's reserve artillery and munitions store was also at Lewes.

It was intended that the Spanish landing would be met only by local forces with the main English armies concentrated further inland. It has been estimated that in the south and south-west the shoreline would be held by some 21,000 local militia, armed with whatever weapons they might possess. The Elizabethan militia was intended to be a formation of all able-bodied males between the ages of 16 to 60. These men had to be prepared to turn out in the defence of their shire at an hour's warning. In each district a number of men were given military training.

These "trained bands" were well-armed and were the backbone of the local defence force. In Sussex there were supposed to have been 2,000 trained men. Of these, 800 were to have carried firearms and the remainder equipped with halberds or pikes. The bow was still considered a weapon of war though its place on the battlefield was being usurped by the matchlock musket.

To protect the south-east and the Thames estuary two small armies, one of 12,000 men and the other of 6,000 men, were to be stationed at Tilbury and Sandwich respectively. Away from these coasts a force of some 27,000 to 34,000 men from the trained bands of the counties would be assembled and another army, 36,000 strong, would be held in reserve to protect the Queen. This last body would be composed of men from the court, from the City of London and the Home Counties. Sussex was expected to find 260 horse and 4,000 foot of which 2,500 were sent to join the main army in the interior. Against these numbers Philip sent 130 ships with 30,000 men who would join forces with the Duke of Parma's 30,000 troops waiting on the Flemish coast. [14]

The Sussex militia were first assembled in the summer of 1586 when fifty ships were sighted off Brighton. Lord Brockhurst responded immediately by bringing together 1,600 men between Brighton and Rottingdean. They camped out on the edge of the Downs that night and they were joined by more men the next day. It proved to be a false alarm as did a similar scare the following summer when horsemen were placed along the coast after reports that an invasion fleet was approaching through the Channel.

With the prospect of invasion becoming increasingly likely Buckhurst was ordered by the Privy Council to round up all "recusants". A recusant is someone who refuses to attend their parish church which effectively meant, and was intended to mean, all Roman Catholics. They were to be placed in the care of the clergy or other people of rank, but if this was not possible the Catholics were to be jailed.

From the outset the Armada ran into difficulties. Storms delayed its departure and further bad weather struck the great fleet before it had even left Spanish waters. Eventually, on the morning of 19 July 1588, the Armada passed the Lizard to head

The medieval gate-tower and moat of Michelham Priory. The Priory is situated to the east of Upper Dicker on the road towards Hailsham, (TQ 558093). (By kind permission of the Director of Michelham Priory and the Sussex Archaeological Society).

up the Channel. The warning beacons were lit: "Swift to East and swift to West the ghastly war-flame spread," a contemporary poem ran. "High on St. Michael's Mount it shone: it shone on Beachy Head." [15]

The English fleet put to sea and the following night slipped round the Armada to place itself windward of the Spanish vessels. Though outnumbered, the English could now control the coming battle. Amongst Lord Howard's ships was a vessel from Rye. The 60-ton vessel *William* was hired from a French privateer and was manned by fifty-eight sailors captained by William Coxson. Four cannon from Rye were added to whatever armament the ship already carried. Another ship, the *Ann Bonaventure* of 70-tons and a crew of forty-nine, was supplied jointly by Hastings and Winchelsea. [16] A third ship from Sussex was provided by Lord Howard with the cost being shared by all six rapes of the county. Hundreds of other sailors were recruited from the Sussex ports to fight with the navy, leaving some parts of the coast dangerously short of defenders.

For the next five days the two fleets fought periodically. The Armada moved in a crescent, or concave, formation, covering a distance of seven miles, with the largest ships at the tips of the crescent. It is often assumed that the battle in the Channel was conducted by an overwhelmingly large number of big Spanish galleons against a weaker force of small, but more manoeuvrable, English warships. The reality was far more complicated. The disparity in numbers was not very great, with the combined fleets of Howard and Sir Francis Drake producing a total of only twenty to thirty less vessels than the Spaniards. In general the tonnage of the ships of the two nations was also roughly the same but the English vessels were of a far more modern design and carried a heavier weight of cannon.

The success of the Spanish land armies meant that the military predominated over the navy to such an extent that their ships were manned by three soldiers to every sailor. In the English ships there were three sailors to every soldier. The English ships did not dare approach too close to the Spanish vessels packed with soldiers for fear of being boarded but their guns, which far out-distanced the Spanish cannon, could inflict little damage upon the stout hulls of the Armada from long range.

On the 25th the Armada passed Selesy Bill and Buckhurst was ordered to see that the militia was mustered and posted at the chosen places along the coast and at important points of communication throughout the county. But by the 26th, the Spaniards had reached Beachy Head and it seemed unlikely that the great fleet would attempt a landfall in Sussex. With day after day of running battles the English fleet soon became desperately short of powder and shot. Buckhurst was ordered to furnish Lord Howard with as much ammunition and food as the ships required. Gunpowder from the Lewes arsenal was sent down the Ouse to Newhaven and then shipped out to Howard's supply vessels. Hastings, assisted by Pevensey, Winchelsea and Seaford, also helped to keep the fleet supplied.

On the 27th, the Armada sailed past Rye and, four days later, Buckhurst allowed the militia to stand down.

In the fighting the Spaniards lost just three ships, but these were amongst their most important galleons and their loss seriously affected the morale of the fleet. By the 28th, the Armada, damaged but still largely intact, was approaching Dover where the rest of the Royal Navy, under Seymour, was guarding the straights, waiting for this very moment.

The Armada, its numerical advantage now lost, anchored in the Calais Roads to await news from the Duke of Parma. Despite ample notice of the Armada's approach, the Duke's troops were not ready to embark and Parma declared that it would be two more weeks before his men could join the invasion fleet. Medina Sidonia knew that he could not remain at anchor for such a period of time with the English fleet able to attack the stationary Spanish vessels at will. With the Spanish ships packed close together under the Calais defences they presented an ideal target for fireships. This was a common naval tactic and a highly effective one. At midnight on 7 August, eight fireships sailed into Calais. Although the Spaniards had been expecting just such an attack, they cut their anchors and put out to sea in utter confusion.

Herstmonceux Castle. The castle is signposted from the A271 to the east of Herstmonceux village, (TQ 646104).

The following day the English fleet attacked the broken and disorganised Armada at the Battle of Gravelines. It was the final battle of the campaign. With little possibility of reaching Parma's men at Dunkirk, and with his ships damaged and his men discouraged, Medina Sidonia turned for the north to round Scotland and return through the North Atlantic to Spain. Of the 130 or so ships that set sail from Corunna in July almost half were lost. [17]

Almost 100 years after the defeat of the great Armada, the "Glorious " Revolution of 1688, which put a Dutch Protestant monarch (William of Orange) on the English throne, led to further trouble with Catholic Europe. On 30 June 1690, a powerful French fleet of seventy-eight men-of-war plus twenty-two fire-ships, met a combined Anglo-Dutch force off Beachy Head.

Despite the fact that the allied fleet numbered just fifty-six vessels, it was the Dutch and British ships which attacked first. The battle raged all day until the wind dropped late in the afternoon. During the night the allied fleet - commanded by Lord Torrington - decided to retire. The French gave pursuit the next day and one English ship, *Anne*, was driven onto the shore at Winchelsea where it was attacked by French fire-ships. The fleet escaped eastwards but allied losses amounted to eight ships and hundreds of men. The Battle of Beachy Head was, without question, a defeat for the Royal Navy and Lord Torrington was duly sent to the Tower and court marshalled. [18]

6
King Against Country
The English Civil War in Sussex

The English nation, divided by religion and loyalty, drifted reluctantly into civil war in 1642. It is hard to say whether it was King Charles I or his political opponents that first threw down the gauntlet. Certainly Charles, in trying to raise revenue for his wars against France and Spain, had imposed taxes in defiance of Parliament. His flagrant disregard for the wishes of his subjects, coupled with religious upheaval and mis-management of the economy, drove many of the most powerful men in the country to oppose him. Though there were many stated reasons for the Civil War of the seventeenth century, in reality it was a revival of the baronnial wars that had halted so abruptly at Evesham. Once again a weak king had tried to over-extend his authority. The democratic principles established after de Montfort's victory at Lewes, limited though they were, had been preserved by Edward I and the great Tudor monarchs that had followed him. Charles I was foolish enough to challenge those principles. His belief in the Divine Right of Kings to rule as they saw fit was the real issue upon which the country went to war. Charles I would not renounce this right, and it cost him his life. Though the monarchy was ultimately restored, the point had been made. Charles II was a constitutional monarch, as would be his successors.

The final descent into war began on 4 January 1642, when Charles tried to arrest five leading Members of Parliament for treason. In response Parliament took control of the Navy and began to raise an army. Though negotiations continued between the King and his opponents for some months, both sides prepared for war. Eventually, on 22 August, the King raised the Royal Standard at Nottingham and hostilities formally commenced.

Sussex saw none of the great battles of the English Civil War and its skirmishes and sieges were small affairs. Yet there was plenty of fighting between Royalist and Roundhead and the occupation of Sussex, with its many cannon foundries, was of considerable importance to both sides.

It is usually stated that Sussex, whilst generally Puritan in its ideology, was divided between a Parliamentary east and a Royalist west. In reality, the picture was far more complicated than this and supporters of both sides could be found throughout the county. Neither was there a distinct class divide, though it is true that most Royalists tended to be men of rank - many of the wealthiest landowners also supported the Parliamentary cause. At the outbreak of hostilities Sussex had twenty-eight Members of Parliament of which eleven could be considered Royalists and seventeen Parliamentarians. [1]

From the outset both sides tried to seize control of the militia trained bands and the store of weapons and ammunition in each county. The King ordered a "Commissions of Array" to bring the militia under his authority and Parliament did the same through a Militia Ordinance Act. At the county town of Chichester an order from Charles I banning the Militia Ordinance was read by the Mayor. This was soon followed, on 19 August, by the county Recorder, Christopher Lewknor, and other influential men, demanding the city's arsenal for the King's service. An officer of the trained bands, Captain Chittey, refused to hand over the magazine and he mounted a strong guard of militia over the military stores. Five days later the people of Chichester, organised by William Cawley, one of the Members of Parliament for Midhurst, declared themselves in support of Parliament. This did not stop local Royalist sympathisers from trying to rally support and they raised a body of light cavalry which drilled each day in the Cathedral Close. Despite the tensions within the city the opposing sides did not descend into actual armed conflict.

For the next few months the Puritans' control of Chichester and the rest of Sussex went unchallenged but in October Parliament ordered the leading Sussex MPs to put the county into a state of defence in readiness for a Royalist attack. This was because the King, at the head of a large army, was threatening to march upon London. A worried Parliament also demanded that all anti-Parliamentarians in Sussex should be disarmed. This pushed the Royalists into action. On 15 November, Royalist forces, led by the Sheriff of Sussex, Edward Ford, gathered in Chichester and took control of the city without a fight. Ford ordered the trained bands to present themselves outside the city the next morning. Ford, accompanied by 100 Royalist horsemen, met the militia half a mile beyond the walls of Chichester and marched them into the city. Once inside the walls, Ford ordered the trained bands to put down their arms which, surprisingly, they appear to have done without dispute. Captain Chittey was removed from his command and was replaced by the Royalist Sir John Morely. So, despite strong Parliamentary popular support in and around Chichester, the city had become a Royalist stronghold without a shot having been fired in anger.

The Parliamentarians' response was swift and effective. Sir William Waller, one of Parliament's most successful generals, marched upon Chichester at the head of around 6,000 men. Waller had recently captured Portsmouth from the Royalists and his main force approached Chichester along the coast road through Havant.

Despite having been informed of Waller's advance, Ford intended to follow up his success at Chichester with the capture of Lewes Castle. He ordered all men capable of bearing arms to join him under pain of death and of having their houses burnt. With an increased, but reluctant, body of men he moved upon Lewes but was met at Haywards Heath by a smaller Parliamentary force. The Puritans attacked Ford's men, probably on the high ground where the church now stands which was then open heath. [2] The combat continued for an hour until reinforcements arrived from the east and completely routed the Royalists. Ford's unwilling followers threw down their arms and ran, the Royalists suffering not less than 200 casualties.

Ford and his supporters retreated back to Chichester and prepared to face Waller. As the Parliamentarian army neared the city Waller despatched a small force to capture Arundel. The great Castle, regarded in Tudor times as being the most powerful in the country, [3] was defended by only 100 men and the Earl of Arundel was out of the country at the outbreak of hostilities. If adequately garrisoned and provisioned Arundel Castle could have been rendered virtually impregnable but when the main gate was blown in and the defenders taken by surprise this magnificent Royalist fortification, along with 100 horses and a store of weapons, was seized without the loss of a single man.

Waller's force arrived before Chichester on 21 December 1642, after a clash with a party of Royalists in which it is said that 200 of the King's supporters were killed for the loss of just forty Parliamentary troops. Waller was joined by the Sussex trained bands who were determined to regain their arms and, no doubt, their credibility. It was soon made clear to Waller, however, that the Royalists were not overawed by the strength of his forces because as soon as the Parliament's army arrived outside the walls of the city the defenders mounted a sortie. The attack was driven back into the city with the loss of one man killed and another taken prisoner.

The city's main fortification was still the old Roman walls and the place could not be expected to withstand a full-scale siege for more than a few days. As soon as the Parliamentarians arrived (known as Roundheads because of the close-cropped hair of their London apprentice-boy soldiers) they began constructing siege batteries on a hill known as The Broyle which overlooked the city walls. The following day, 22 December, Waller summoned the garrison to surrender.

Waller's terms were that Edward Ford and all Catholics were to be handed over as prisoners, the soldiers were to lay down their weapons and leave the city, and the officers were to give a pledge that they would never again take up arms against Parliament. Though the garrison was prepared to offer up all the "Papists" the rest of Waller's terms were rejected and on the 23rd the siege guns opened fire, though to little effect. The defenders resisted by mounting cannon on top of the former castle motte which were able to fire over the walls at the attackers.

Surprisingly, the walls seem to have withstood the bombardment and it was only against the city's gates that progress was made. The gates could only be approached through the suburbs and on the 24th the besiegers occupied the houses by the west gate. The garrison responded by setting fire to some of the houses next to the gate and the attackers had to withdraw. The same situation developed at the east gate and again fire was used to dislodge the besiegers. For the next two days the Parliamentarians attacked the city from all sides yet it was not until Boxing Day that the besiegers had cleared the suburbs and had brought their cannon to within 100 yards of the north gate where they could fire into the market place.

A reinforcement of troops from Arundel under Colonel Roberts had joined Waller and had taken control of the ground opposite the south gate. It was obvious that the city could not hold back the besiegers for much longer. With the attackers forcing an entry through the postern which opened into the Deanery, coupled with clear preparations for simultaneous attacks upon the east and west gates, the garrison offered to surrender on terms. But Waller was no longer willing to negotiate and the garrison was left with the choice of unconditional surrender or a fight to the death. They chose to capitulate.

Chichester had delayed Waller for just eight days. Many of the leading Sussex Royalists were taken prisoner, including Sir Edward Ford, and the county came under Parliament's undisputed control. The prisoners included seventeen captains, thirteen lieutenants and eight ensigns along with around 400 dragoons and 300 to 400 infantry. The captives were marched of to London, some being conveyed to the capital by ship from Chichester Harbour. Chichester remained a Parliamentary-garrisoned city with Colonel Anthony Stapely as its governor until March 1646 when the guns were removed to Arundel.

There is no doubt that the control of Sussex by Parliament brought considerable benefits to their war effort nationally. At this time there were around twenty-seven furnaces in Sussex, the majority of which made guns and shot - the most important being the Royal Foundries in St. Leonard's Forest. In addition there were forty-two forges or iron-mills. [4] It was in Sussex - at Buxted near Uckfield in 1543 - that the first cannon had been cast as a single piece in England. Before that event cannon had been made by strips of iron bound together by iron hoops. For the subsequent 200 years the gun foundries of the Weald were the most important in the country. The Sussex-made guns were regarded as being the finest and cheapest in Europe and laws were passed to prevent the unlicensed export of these weapons to hostile countries. [5]

The occupation of Sussex and its ports by Parliamentarian troops also meant that one of the potential avenues through which Charles might receive financial and military assistance from France was sealed off. Sussex's position on the coast helped Parliament's cause in July 1644 when a Puritan force under the Earl of Essex needed money to pay his troops but the occupation of intervening counties by Royalists prevented any overland communication. The money, £20,000, was sent from London to Arundel and Chichester from where it was shipped round the coast to Devon.

Since the end of the Hundred Years War, England had known many years of relative peace. In 1642 there was no standing army and few soldiers with any fighting experience. The principle military forces in England at the start of the war were the trained bands of local county militia. However, these were not obliged, nor usually willing, to serve beyond the boundaries of their own county. Though the trained bands were the best infantry that either side possessed, the localised nature of their enlistment meant that they could not be used in country-wide campaigns and the opposing armies resorted to recruitment and impressment. As a result many men, other than those who were motivated by personal beliefs or convictions, could be induced to change sides, depending on the current fortunes of the opposing armies.

Apart from the trained bands the regiments of foot and horse in both armies were raised for a specific engagement or campaign and were disbanded when hostilities were concluded. This changed with Parliament's creation of the "New Model" Army in which regiments became permanent establishments, laying down the foundations of the modern British Army. In military terms, the decision of 27 January 1645 to create a regular standing army was the most significant of the entire conflict and it won the war for Parliament. At its inception Sussex was directed to supply 600 of their finest men, and a large sum of money, for this service.

The principle infantry weapon of the English Civil War was the matchlock musket. These were large and cumbersome implements with a barrel length of up to four and a half feet. There was no common pattern and no standard calibre. The effective range of a smoothbore musket was extremely limited but at close quarters a musket volley could be devastating. The bayonet had not been invented at the time of the Civil War and musketeers were easy prey to well-mounted cavalry. To defend the musketeers from cavalry attacks a proportion of the infantry in each regiment were armed with pikes. These were iron-headed spears mounted on wooden (ash) poles between fifteen and eighteen feet long. Pikes were not only designed to defend the musketeers but were also used offensively and the "push of pikes" could decide the battle. The secondary weapon of both musketeers and pikemen was the sword.

The cavalry were armed with swords and, when they could be procured, pistols and short-barrelled muskets called carbines. In the main the cavalry wore buff leather coats with steel breast plates and back plates, plus an open-faced steel helmet. Some also had a steel gauntlet to protect their bridle hand and steel thigh-guards called tassets. Complete suits of armour were expensive and heavy and were a rare sight on the Civil War battlefields.

A recent development was the dragoon, or mounted infantryman. Armed and equipped as musketeers these highly mobile troops were ideal for scouting and as advanced or rear guards.

Pikemen usually wore buff coats with breast and back plates, helmets and, frequently, tassets. Musketeers were not armoured and usually wore just their buff coats and a wide-brimmed hat. The ubiquitous buff coat was a thick ox hide sleeveless jacket with a skirt that covered the thighs. It could resist sword cuts and bullets fired from long range.

Artillery of the 17th Century was of limited value on the battlefield as the cannon were difficult to manoeuvre and could only maintain a very slow rate of fire (eight to ten rounds per hour). It was in siege warfare that artillery was most effective. There were two basic types of ordnance, the cannon and the mortar. Cannon threw solid, iron balls weighing up to sixty-three pounds, in a relatively flat trajectory, and were used to batter down the walls of a castle. Mortars fired explosive shells in a high trajectory over the battlements to fall inside the castle.[6]

....

For almost twelve months Parliament's hold upon Sussex remained unbroken despite occasional attacks by Royalist forces. A Cavalier raid on Petworth House had captured twenty Parliamentarian cavalry who were taken back to Oxford. South Harting, near the Hampshire border, had also witnessed a skirmish in which 120 men of the Earl of Crawfurd's Regiment drove off some 200 Parliamentarian dragoons. Both sides lost only a handful of men.

Waller was appointed Major-General of the Association of Sussex, Kent and Surrey, with Farnham becoming his base of operations. The departure of Waller's forces to Farnham allowed the Royalists troops in Hampshire to invade Sussex, and in December 1643 the county was drawn into the main theatre of the war. King Charles had planned a combined advance upon London from the north, and from the south through Sussex and Surrey.

The southern attack was to be delivered by Sir Ralph Hopton, who had been the first man to oppose the King with force the previous year but was now an important Royalist general. Hopton's route through Sussex was by Harting and Marden and then over the Downs to Arundel. To keep open his line of communication Hopton garrisoned Harting Place and Edward

Ford's regiment of horse was quartered at his father's house of Uppark to guard the passes through the Downs.

Detachments of cavalry from Hopton's force were sent to capture the great country houses of Petworth, Cowdray and Stanstead. In those days Stanstead was a castellated building with a turreted gateway and the first Royalist assault was driven off. After a sharp fight, however, this fine old house fell to the attackers.

Hopton's advance guard, led by the irrepressible Edward Ford, reached Arundel on 6 December. Ford captured the town and laid siege to the castle. The Parliamentary garrison was strong enough to hold the powerful fortifications against Hopton's force of only 5,500 men. However, Arundel had not expected an attack. Sussex's best defence was its inaccessibility but heavy frosts had hardened the normally muddy roads and Hopton's rapid march caught the Parliamentarians unprepared. The Castle was not provisioned for a prolonged investment and the garrison's reserves of ammunition were very limited.

News of Hopton's arrival at Arundel spread quickly throughout the county. Measures were immediately taken to garrison Bramber Castle and strengthen its fortifications. Shoreham, whose Castle has long since disappeared, was also placed in a state of defence with six large cannon from Rye and timber and lead from the ruined Castle at Camber. But before any help could be offered to Arundel the garrison surrendered.

From Arundel Hopton's forces then moved eastwards and Colonel Morely, with as many men as he could muster, decided to hold the line of the Adur. The Royalists attacked Bramber Castle which was held by a small Puritan unit under the command of Captain James Temple. Unlike Arundel, Bramber held out. A second attempt to force the passage of the Adur by the Royalists at Bramber bridge was also driven off. [7]

Though Morely had prevented Hopton from moving into eastern Sussex, the county west of the Adur was firmly in Royalists hands including the great houses of Cowdray, Petworth

Cowdray House. The ruins of this fortified manor house are only open to the public at specified times. They can be viewed from a public footpath that leads of the main A272 road, (SU 892217).

and Stanstead, as well as Arundel Castle. It was time for Waller to intervene.

He set off from Farnham on Sunday 17 December, marching by way of Haslemere and Midhurst. Hoping to take the garrison of Cowdray House by surprise, he sent two regiments of cavalry to block the roads and surround the house. The Royalist garrison, of four troops of horse and 100 foot, learnt of Waller's advance and the men escaped to Arundel. Petworth, where Hopton had his headquarters, was Waller's next target but again the Cavaliers escaped, with Hopton making his way to Winchester and others joining the garrison of Arundel Castle.

The Castle was occupied by around 1,100 men including the troops from Cowdray and Petworth. Waller, with 6,000 men, camped his army within a mile of Arundel on the evening of Tuesday the 19th. At dawn the following morning Waller reconnoitred the town. He found that Hopton had surrounded the place with earthworks which had to be taken before the Parliamentarians could approach the Castle. After a preliminary artillery bombardment Waller delivered simultaneous attacks upon the north and south-west of the town and after about thirty minutes of fighting seized the outworks and captured some eighty men.

Though the Royalist cavalry made a sortie from the Castle, the town was taken by the Parliamentarians, and the Cavaliers were driven back into the Castle. Waller took another sixty prisoners in the town.

On 21 December, Morely's regiment joined the besieging forces as well as a further 600 cavalry which were sent from the Earl of Essex. The weather, which had been fine and frosty for many days, now broke and the town was lashed by violent rain storms. Where possible the besieging troops were billeted in the houses of the town but this meant that they were within range of marksmen posted in the upper part of the Castle. In an attempt to counter the marksmen two light field pieces called "saker drakes" were hauled up to the tower of Arundel church during the night and at first light they, along with a unit of musketeers, poured a heavy fire upon the battlements.

Yet more Roundhead reinforcements were received, this time from Kent, in the form of a regiment of cavalry and another of foot. The odds against the Royalists were becoming greater by the day and many members of the garrison deserted what was clearly a lost cause. The water supply to the Castle came from Swanbourne Lake and the besiegers began draining off the water from the lake. By Saturday 23 December, this had been completed and the garrison had only the water remaining in the Castle wells.

The situation was becoming desperate for the defenders but they were able to keep in communication with Hopton (even though one messenger was caught and hanged on the bridge within sight of the Castle) via a small boat upon which the messengers crossed the Arun. Despite commanding less than 3,000 men, Hopton marched from Winchester to the relief of Arundel on 27 December.

When news of Hopton's approach reached Waller he left just 1,500 men to continue the siege and he moved to meet the Royalists with the rest of his force. The opposing armies met on the 29th at West Dean, four miles north of Chichester. This was the largest gathering of hostile forces on Sussex soil since the Battle of Lewes. But the advantage in numbers was entirely in favour of the Parliamentarians and Hopton, after a brief skirmish, sensibly withdrew.

After Hopton had failed to relieve the garrison, the Royalists offered to surrender on terms. Waller, whose position was now unassailable, would not negotiate. With some heavy guns that he had received from Portsmouth, Waller began to bombard the Castle on 4 January. The garrison was by this time reduced to an allowance of meat and two spoons of wheat per man per day and many inside the walls had fallen ill.

The next day three commissioners were sent out from the Castle to arrange terms of surrender and at approximately 09.00 hours on 6 January 1644, Arundel Castle was surrendered to Parliament. The siege had lasted seventeen days.

Waller took possession of around 200 horses, 2,000 weapons, twenty barrels of gunpowder and some £4,000. More than 1,000 soldiers, including about 100 officers and nineteen colours were taken. Edward Ford was treated with surprising leniency by Parliament, merely being branded as "incapable of any employment."

The beautifully restored castle at Arundel. Note the large, round keep in the centre of the Castle and the bailey on either side, (TQ 017074). (Reproduced by kind permission of His Grace The Duke of Norfolk).

Arundel and its Castle had suffered severely from both Hopton's and Waller's attacks. Shortly after the siege a visitor to Arundel described the place as "a most dismal sight: the town being depopulated, all the windows broken with the great guns, and the soldiers making stables in all the shops". [8] During the siege many of the besiegers as well as the besieged died of a fever, probably typhus. The Castle was "slighted" in 1649 and left roofless and ruined. Never again would this once-mighty fortification challenge the authority of Parliament.

Waller set about securing Sussex. The garrison of Chichester was increased to 800 men and a large magazine, which included 100 barrels of gunpowder, was formed in Arundel Castle. More troops were also raised through an ordinance of 31 March 1644, which called for 3,000 foot, 1,200 horse and 500 dragoons from Hampshire, Surrey, Sussex and Kent.

During the summer of 1644, Colonel Morley with six companies of men from Sussex assisted in the siege of Basing House, the fortified residence of the Marquis of Winchester, in Hampshire. Later in the year Sussex troops also served as far afield as Dorset. But a large body of Royalists under Sir George Goring was active in the eastern areas of Hampshire, and Parliament ordered 500 dragoons from Kent, Sussex and Surrey to join a force of 1,000 foot from Reading which was to defend the Sussex border. At the same time the trained bands were ordered up to garrison Chichester and Arundel.

Meanwhile the remarkable siege of Basing House continued and Sussex was ordered to find 400 more men to support the besiegers. Muskets and horses were also taken from the Sussex magazines for the siege. The continual drain upon the resources of the ordinary people, the plundering of the troops and the requisitions of Parliament, drove the people of the southern counties into revolt. Known as the Clubmen because their weapons were clubs and agricultural implements, the movement began in Wiltshire and Dorset and soon spread to Hampshire and Sussex. A thousand Clubmen met at Rowkeshill [9] near Chichester at the middle of September and a call went out for a further meeting at Bury Hill. This was pre-empted by a Major Young who attacked a number of Clubmen at Walberton with some forty infantry and ten horse, killing one man and causing the rest to flee. This was followed by the capture of the leading Clubmen and the movement lost momentum. However, resistance to Parliament's demands for men and money continued. Taxes went unpaid throughout the county and few men responded the call for reinforcements to the New Model Army.

Within weeks of the outbreak of hostilities in 1642, Parliament declared that the cost of the war would be borne by those who supported the King and on 15 October the Lords went one step further by announcing that anyone who refused to help the Parliamentary cause with money would be imprisoned and their goods sequestered. In January 1644, Parliament, in the hope of persuading Royalists to abandon their support for Charles, allowed those that had followed the King to pay a fine and get their property back if they renounced their allegiance to the Crown. Many leading Royalists took this opportunity of saving their estates. The fines, however, were often nothing short of extortionate and in many cases long legal battles followed. Sir John Goring of Amberley had repeatedly refused to accept Parliament's right to extract money for the war and he encouraged the local people to place their goods and valuables in his castle where they would be safe from the grasp of the Parliamentarians. This was open defiance and could not be ignored by Waller. He marched the five miles from Arundel and attacked Amberley Castle. Though the walls of the Castle show no signs of having suffered heavy bombardment, Waller forced his way into the castle and seized Goring. Waller destroyed the internal buildings of the Castle and rendered it defenceless by pulling down its parapet.

With the eventual fall of Basing House, after the longest siege of the war, the threat of Civil War was removed from the Sussex borders. Elsewhere the King's fortunes continued to ebb and following his defeats at Marston Moor and Naseby, Charles fled to Scotland where he was captured and handed over to his enemies. The First Civil War was over.

What followed was a sordid and unnecessary affair. Charles

A gun emplacement and magazine of the 19th century Lower Battery at Newhaven, which is now adjacent to the West Beach car park, (TQ 448001).

however, the Duke of York ordered the battery to be fully manned and supported by at least 200 troops. The East Bank Battery remained in service until 1835.

The 'blockhouse' and gun garden at Brighton were still standing, though both of these were being undermined by coastal erosion. There was also a small fort at Hastings which mounted eleven 12-pounders, but between Brighton and Hastings there were no significant defences at all. It was in 1759, therefore, that the Board of Ordnance ordered the construction of batteries in Seaford Bay. [3]

At Newhaven a battery was established on Castle Hill overlooking Newhaven harbour. It housed five 12-pounder cannon and included a powder magazine and barracks. To cover the flat ground between the estuary of the Ouse and Seaford Head two further batteries were built. The first was on Blatchington Down and was armed with five 24-pounders. The second, of five 12-pounders, was on Seaford beach in front of the town. Both of these batteries also had powder magazines and barracks for the gunners. In the same year the decaying Brighton defences were replaced by the Great East Street Battery. This work held twenty antique 20-pounder cannon.

Strangely all these batteries were not under the jurisdiction of the military. The Master Gunner, who was the officer in charge

The remains of the fort at Littlehampton that can be seen today, (TQ 027012). Just visible beneath the undergrowth is the loop-holed Carnot Wall and part of a caponnier. Access is provided by the Rope Walk along the western bank of the River Arun.

of each battery, was a civilian as was his second in command, though he was also a trained gunner. These were both full-time posts paid for by the Government. Until the middle of the 18th century the cost of maintaining and manning coastal defences had to be borne locally. At Brighton, for instance, a quarter of the profit from each boat on the beach had to go towards the purchase of powder and shot for the gun batteries.

The rest of the personnel were local volunteers, often old soldiers.

Though France and her allies amassed an armada of flat-bottomed boats along the coast from St. Malo to Dunkirk the Royal Navy kept the enemy fleet blockaded in its own harbours. Twice in 1759, however, the French were able to slip through the blockades with the intention of rounding up the invasion craft and escorting them across the Channel. But on both occasions the French were followed and intercepted by the Royal Navy and the French fleets of Brest and Toulon were eventually caught and destroyed in Quiberon Bay.

A little over thirty years after the destruction of the Toulon fleet at Quiberon Bay, France once again threatened to invade southern England. This was the time of the French Revolution and its greatest military leader, Napoleon Bonaparte.

In the summer (i.e. the invasion season) of both 1793 and 1794, huge tented camps were formed at Brighton. Accommodating 10-15,000 troops, the 1793 camp was established along the sea front running westwards for over a mile from the present-day Regency Square. The 1794 camp was pitched on Race Hill. Elaborate training exercises and mock battles, with the Prince of Wales happily playing his part as Colonel of the 10th Dragoons, were a frequent spectacle in and around Brighton at this time. [4]

A signal station, more correctly called a telegraph, was also sited on Race Hill. Messages could be sent and received to and from the adjacent stations at Seaford in the east and Shoreham to the west. These telegraphs were part of a network of signal stations which the Admiralty built on the coast to allow communications both out to the ships of the Royal Navy and along the coast. Sixteen of these stations were in Sussex. [5]

Permanent barracks were later built at Brighton with one for infantry being raised opposite the stables of the Royal Pavilion and another for cavalry along the Lewes Road. At Chichester in the Broyle Road, the Roussillion Barracks were built to accommodate 1,500 men, and at nearby Selsey a wooden barracks housed a further 300 soldiers. Shoreham, Southwick, Steyning, Worthing, Littlehampton, Arundel and Bognor Regis all had barracks during the Napoleonic Wars.

The result of further invasion scares beginning in 1795 and reaching a climax between 1803 to 1805, led to the complete militarisation of the south coast. Not only was there a massive programme of re-fortification but large numbers of troops were stationed in the south and substantial garrisons established at every important position along the coast.

Amongst the earliest of these fortifications were the batteries at Langney Point to the east of Eastbourne. On this flat and exposed beach two substantial forts were erected in 1795.

Each armed with six captured French 24-pounders, the batteries were enclosed at the rear with loop-holed walls and a ditch. [6] Altogether there were ten batteries in Sussex, the others being the existing ones at Rye, Hastings, Eastbourne, Seaford, Blatchington, Newhaven, Brighton and Littlehampton. The companies raised locally to serve these batteries were intended to consist of one captain, two lieutenants and sixty men, of whom at least one third were armed with muskets and the rest with pikes. [7]

In 1801, the Commander-in-Chief of the army, the Duke of York, toured the south coast and drew up his "Information and Instructions for Commanding Generals and Others" detailing his plans for the defence of London and the south. The principle behind his plan was that there would be no attempt to defend the coastline. There were so many likely landing places, the Duke reckoned, that it would be impossible to predict where the French would attack. He proposed, therefore, to concentrate his forces at selected points. In West Sussex those points were at North Mundham to protect Chichester and Pagham Harbour; at Warningcamp to defend the Arun valley; at Highdown Hill to watch the coast between Worthing and Shoreham, and on Hollingbury Hill to cover Brighton.

If the invaders broke through, or outflanked, these concentration points, the defenders would fall back to a second line of rallying posts. These were to be at Shermanbury, Stopham, Houghton and Westbourne near the Hampshire border. If this second line was over-run the troops would retreat to Horsham and Guildford to defend the roads through the North Downs leading to London

To impede the French advance the countryside was to be

Two gun pivots which once formed part of the defensive armament of the Langney Redoubt. These are standing at the end of the sea-front promenade at Langney Point, Eastbourne, (TQ 642011).

The scant remains of a gun emplacement from the Langney Redoubt, situated at the end of the promenade at Langney Point.

abandoned and everything that might be useful to the enemy was to be removed or ruined. Livestock and all means of conveyance (carts, horses and boats) were to be driven inland and crops and magazines were to be destroyed.

A section of the Royal Military Canal at Pett Level, (TQ 894139).

The low-lying areas of the Romney Marsh and the Pett and Pevensey Levels were to be flooded by opening the sluice gates of the drainage ditches and by breaching the sea wall. [8] Roads would be blocked or broken up whilst the British cavalry harried the flanks of the advancing invaders.

For a brief period of time Britain and France were at peace but with the renewal of hostilities in 1803, the subject of coastal defence was once again thrust onto the Government's agenda. Napoleon saw Britain as the principle obstacle in his attempt at European, and possibly even world, domination. He formed a vast camp at Boulogne where 100,000 men assembled under the optimistic title of "The Army of England". Only the Royal Navy, and the uncertain waters of the Channel, stood between Napoleon and the Kent and Sussex coasts.

In the autumn of 1804 the Government decided to build an entire series of permanent defences along the coast from Dover to Beachy Head. Eventually these defences were extended to run from Suffolk to Sussex and numbered no less than 103 towers and redoubts and included a massive defensive ditch from below Winchelsea to Hythe in Kent.

The area of land encompassed by this defensive ditch, which became known as the Royal Military Canal, was considered to be the most vulnerable point along the entire south coast. The canal was to begin at Shorncliff above Hythe and terminate at Cliff End to the north-east of Hastings, running for a distance of twenty-eight miles and embracing the flat, low-lying regions of Romney Marsh and Pett Level.

Along the northern bank of the canal a parapet was formed from the earth excavated during the digging of the canal. In the event of an invasion, defending infantry and artillery would be able to fire over the parapet. The canal was built with a profile similar to a 19th century fort, incorporating salient angles to allow flanking, or enfilade fire, along the face of the parapet. Behind the protection of the parapet was a road to enable the safe and rapid transfer of troops along the line to any threatened point. Originally it was suggested that the canal should be sixty-two feet wide at the surface, forty-four feet wide at the bottom and nine feet deep. The adjoining parapet was to be thirty-five feet wide and the accompanying road thirty feet.

On 30 October 1804, the first ground was broken at Shorncliffe. The project was under the supervision of a civilian engineer, John Rennie, who had been responsible for the construction of the London and Waterloo bridges. It was intended that the canal would be completed by June of the following year, but by May 1805 only six miles of ditch had been dug. Amid much acrimony the contractors were dismissed, Rennie resigned and the work was taken over by the Army.

The Royal Staff Corps established its headquarters at Hythe and took over responsibility for the building programme. Soldiers were used to construct the parapet but civilian labour was still used to dig the canal, and by August more than 1,500 men were hard at work. The ditch was dug by hand, the men possessing only picks and shovels, with the earth being removed by wheelbarrow. Because much of the ground was at or below sea level the ditch was prone to flooding and large steam-driven pumps were in almost constant use. The proposed surface width of sixty-two feet was only accomplished at the eastern end of the canal and along most of its length the canal is only half that distance across. In many parts the required depth of nine feet was not achieved. When the canal was opened in August 1806 the threat of invasion had receded thanks to Nelson's great victory over the French fleet at Trafalgar. [9]

Along the coast on either side of the canal ran the long chain of towers. They were constructed to a design similar to a fort built by the French in Mortella Point, Corsica which had withstood considerable bombardment from British guns in 1793. The "Martello" towers were elliptical in shape with an axis of

An early painting of what appears to be Martello Tower No. 28 at Rye Harbour. Though in poor condition, the tower can be seen adjacent to the car park at the end of Rye Harbour Road, (TQ 942188).

45ft x 42ft at the base and 39ft x 35ft at the top. They stood nearly thirty-three feet high and some were provided with a dry brick-lined ditch some thirty-eight feet wide and sixteen feet deep. The walls were twelve feet thick on the seaward side and seven feet thick on the landward side. [10]

At the bottom of each tower were cisterns to catch rainwater. Above these was the ground floor where the magazine was located. The first floor was the main living area for one officer and twenty-four men. The entrance was also on this level. It was eleven feet above the ground and was reached by a ladder which could be taken up and stored inside the tower. Where the tower had a ditch, access was over a drop bridge.

An internal stone staircase led from the first floor to the gun roof. The single 24-pounder cannon was mounted on a sliding carriage. This carriage was fixed to a traversing platform which was fitted with wheels that ran along metal rails embedded into the masonry below the parapet. With the aid of a central pivot the cannon could be turned and pointed in any direction. To counter the recoil the gun was angled upon a 1 in 12 slope which also helped to run the gun forward again. The gun fired *en barbette* over a thick, stone parapet which also had a firing step for infantry. If the tower stood at a point where the ground might

Martello Tower No. 74 on the sea-front Esplanade at Seaford, (TQ 485985).

Martello Tower No.55, at Norman's Bay, which stands between the seafront properties that back onto the minor road from Pevensey Bay, (TQ 684053).

Caponnier and ditch at the Eastbourne Redoubt. The Redoubt is situated on the promenade to the east of Eastbourne town centre, (TV 623997).

conceal the approach of the enemy the fortress also mounted two 5.5 inch howitzers. Such places in Sussex were the Wish Tower (No.73) which still stands on the cliffs to the west of Eastbourne and nearby Anthony Hill (No.68).

Along the most accessible stretches of the coast the towers were built just 500-600 yards apart, enabling them to be mutually supporting and allowing their guns to form deadly cross-fires. The towers were provided with the resources to withstand a siege and they were utterly impregnable to troops without heavy artillery.

Altogether, 103 towers were built from Aldeburgh in Suffolk to Seaford. The ones on the south coast were numbered from east to west with No.1 at Folkstone to No.74 at Seaford.

Included with the standard towers were three larger forts. At Eastbourne, Dymchurch in Kent and Harwich on the east coast, three circular redoubts were constructed. The Eastbourne Circular Redoubt is 216 feet in diameter and was originally armed with ten 24-pounders and had facilities for a garrison of 400 men. Unlike the Martello Towers it was partially sunk into the ground and was well concealed from the sea. This was to be the principle work along this vulnerable stretch of coastline, supported by the Langney Batteries and Pevensey Levels to the east which could be flooded by the opening of the Pevensey sluices. To the west, of course, are the towering chalk walls of Beachy Head.

The defences of the Sussex coast were under the command of Sir James Pultney who established his headquarters at Eastbourne. The construction of the Martello Towers was a considerable and lengthy operation and with 130,000 French troops waiting at Boulonge for nothing more than a favourable wind to blow their boats across the Channel, immediate measures had to be taken. So Pultney arranged for the construction of "emergency" batteries to be erected around the coast. Situated about 500 yards apart along vulnerable parts of the coast, Pultney had the batteries built with earthen ramparts seven feet high and armed with 24-pounders. These batteries remained in use until the building of the Martello Towers had been completed. Though it is not certain how many of these batteries were constructed, it is known that no less than eighteen were erected in and around Eastbourne alone. Work on the Martello Towers began in March 1804 but by the time the great chain of forts had been built it was 1812 and the fear of invasion was but a distant memory.

The return of France to a Bonapartist regime under Napoleon III, prompted a rush of new defensive works along the south coast. At Littlehampton, Shoreham and Newhaven substantial fortifications were erected in the 1850s.

The new fort at Littlehampton was sited on the west bank of the Arun and was completed in 1854. It was built in the form of a lunette with two flanks and two faces but with an enclosed rear protected by earthworks. Around the work was a dry ditch, twenty-seven feet wide, at the base of which was a loop-holed, twelve feet high, Carnot wall. Three small, open bastions were formed on the three salient angles of the Carnot wall to provide enfilade fire along the ditch. It was armed with three 68-pounder and two 32-pounder smooth-bore cannon and the garrison comprised two infantry officers, one master gunner, and forty-eight other ranks, including six trained gunners. With its own artesian well and magazines, it was capable of a sustained defence, even if attacked from both the land and the sea. [11]

An even stronger fort was built at Shoreham. Though just three years newer than the Littlehampton fort, the Shoreham work incorporated some of the most recent developments in fortification. Its basic design was very similar to the Littlehampton fort but instead of small, open bastions on the Carnot wall, the Shoreham fort had large, fully enclosed carponniers. The fort mounted six 68-pounders sited on dwarf traversing platforms which enabled the guns to command the harbour entrance and the beaches on either side of the Adur estuary. [12]

At Newhaven a new battery was erected at the foot of Castle Hill to supplement the guns of the 1759 battery on top of the hill. The new Lower Battery was armed with six guns to defend the harbour entrance and the approach to West Beach. The 1759 battery remained in use and was re-named the Upper Battery.

Lord Palmerston, the Prime Minister from 1855 to 1865, authorised a Royal Commission to re-examine the whole question of coastal defence. The Commission reported in 1860 and included amongst its proposals was the construction of the

Shoreham Redoubt, showing the loop-holed Carnot wall and caponnier. The redoubt is at the end of Fort Haven at the eastern extremity of Shoreham Beach, (TQ 233045).

largest defensive structure in Sussex to replace the old Upper Battery at Newhaven. The reason why such a massive fortification was required here was that Newhaven was rapidly becoming one of the most important ports in Sussex following the opening of a direct rail line with London (1847) and the development of a cross-Channel steam boat service to France in 1849.

The fort was dug out of the chalk headland overlooking the harbour with the cliffs themselves forming the glacis and the ramparts. Despite occupying almost sixteen acres of ground, it was virtually unidentifiable as a fortification from the sea. The landward sides of the fort were protected by a wide, dry ditch and access to the fort is over a bridge and through a cut in the chalk glacis. The ditch was defended by counterscarp galleries from which both infantry and artillery could fire the length of the ditch.

One of the most remarkable features of the fort is a large caponnier, with sally port, which was built at the foot of the cliffs by the old Lower Battery. Access to the caponnier is via a long tunnel and steps cut through the cliff. With barracks for 245 men and originally armed with nine large-calibre guns, Newhaven Fort was the strongest coastal fortification between Dover and Portsmouth - the Eastbourne Circular Redoubt was now considered to be obsolete. The fort was completed in 1871 and was the first major military structure in Britain to use large quantities of concrete in its construction.

Though the improvement in artillery had made the magazines at the Eastbourne Circular Redoubt vulnerable to attack by naval shipping, the redoubt remained in service and was re-armed, in 1859, with 110-pounders, 68-pounders, and 8-inch muzzle-loading guns. By this time the West Fort at Langney Point had become derelict but the East Fort was modernised with caponniers on the rear walls and re-armed with 68-pounders. This fort was re-named the Langney Redoubt.

Throughout the last decades of the nineteenth century the old gun batteries along the coast were abandoned by the military. The Upper Battery at Newhaven had been incorporated into the Newhaven Fort but the Seaford Battery was washed into the sea in 1860 and the Blatchington Battery was sold off ten years later.

The Langney Redoubt survived until the early years of the twentieth century and the Eastbourne Circular Redoubt still stands today. The latter was disposed of by the Army towards the end of the 19th century, but was re-occupied by the military during World War II.

The improvements in the range and accuracy of ordnance soon made the Littlehampton and Shoreham forts obsolete. Their parapets were too weak and their smooth-bore guns ineffective. Though extensive re-working was proposed, neither fort received any structural improvement. The Littlehampton West Bank Fort was abandoned by the military in 1891 but the Shoreham Redoubt continued to be maintained as a military establishment until after World War I. Shoreham's old ordnance was replaced by three 64-pounder and two 80-pounder rifled guns. The latter remained in service until 1921.

8
The World at War

There was no serious possibility of a German invasion of England during World War I and few measures were considered necessary for the protection of the coast. The defence of the coastline was left in the hands of the Territorial Army. Initially there was no attempt to line the shore with troops. Instead a "Central Force" of nine TA divisions and two Yeomanry divisions was held back from the coast ready to counter any advance inland by an invader. Later this policy was reversed and the troops were moved closer to the coast to prevent the enemy establishing a foothold on the beaches.[1]

The only place in Sussex to receive any defensive armament was Newhaven Fort which was re-armed with two rapid-firing 6-inch guns to combat fast German torpedo boats. The guns were served by men of the Royal Garrison Artillery, assisted by Territorial Army Engineers who manned searchlights situated on the harbour breakwater. Newhaven became a principle embarkation port for stores and munitions shipped out from England to the Western Front.

Large tented camps were formed in the area to accommodate the troops destined for the trenches. Huge camps were formed at Shoreham, Tide Mills and on Chailey Common. Ashdown Forest was also the scene of much military activity during this period with camps at Forest Row, Kidbrooke Park, King's Standing, Camp Hill, Pippingford and St. John's Common. The Forest continued to be used by the military through World War II and even to the present day. [2]

Aerodromes, seaplane bases and airship stations of the Royal Flying Corps, (R.F.C.), and the Royal Naval Air Service were located along the coast. Polegate was the site for one of the earliest non-rigid airship stations. From Polegate the first 'Submarine Scout' airship began patrols along the Channel on 6 July 1915. A year later these craft were replaced with the larger SS Zero airships which could remain in the air for over seventeen hours. By September 1917, six Zeros were operating out of Polegate. The Zero had a crew of three - pilot, observer/gunner and an engineer who sat next to the engine. [3] The airships, known as 'Blimps', were used mainly for spotting German submarines which then operated in considerable numbers in the Channel.

Possibly the most important air-base was at Newhaven. Formed on the East Beach, the RNAS flew seaplane patrols along the coast between Dungeness and the Isle of Wight. Newhaven's four Short 184 seaplanes were armed with a Lewis gun and could carry a maximum bomb load of one 112lb and two 50lb bombs. The other bases in Sussex were at St. Anthony's Eastbourne, Middleton, Goring, and East Preston.

To counter the threat of Zepplin (and later Gotha bomber) raids upon London, No.78 Squadron of the R.F.C. was formed. One flight of this squadron, flying Bristol BE2c and B12 fighters, was based at Telscombe Cliffs. Initially the airfield was operational for just one year from September 1917, but was reactivated for a few months in 1918.

Shoreham Airport was designated as a training airfield and, in 1915, No.3 Reserve Aeroplane Squadron arrived flying Maurice Farman Longhorns. Tangmere airfield was built in 1917 (using German POW labour) and was the base for No.92 Squadron which was equipped with SE 5As, and No.61 Squadron which flew Avro 504s and Bristol F2Bs. Ford airfield was another training station which became operational towards the end of the war. Ford and Tangmere, as well as Southbourne and Rustington, were amongst five sites originally selected as training bases for the United States airforce to fly the huge Handley Page night bombers. [4]

The worrying ease with which German submarines could pass through the Channel prompted the construction, in 1917, of one of the most remarkable structures ever built in Sussex. An anti-submarine barrier was to be laid between the Goodwin Sands and Dunkirk. It was to be strengthened by sixteen enormous concrete gun towers. The first pair of towers, which were to be towed out to sea and then sunk into thirty fathoms of

taken to Sussex for treatment and care, including large numbers of Empire troops. Twenty-five "auxiliary" hospitals were established throughout the county to deal with the influx of thousands of badly injured soldiers. [6]

As in World War I there was little perceived threat of an attack upon Britain at the outbreak of World War II other than

The gun emplacements for the Emergency Coastal Battery at Newhaven located on the cliff top to the west of Newhaven Fort, (TQ 4477001).

water with the towers rising 100 feet above sea-level, were built at Shoreham. Only one was completed by the end of the war and this tower was towed out to the Nab sandbanks east of the Isle of Wight. Now known as the Nab Tower lighthouse, it remains there to this day. [5]

The pounding of the guns on the Western Front could be heard in many areas of Sussex and, because of the county's proximity to the Continent, men wounded in the fighting were

from the air. Such complacency was immediately swept away when the British army was driven from the Continent, being saved from complete annihilation only by the heroics at Dunkirk, (in which many small boats from Sussex played their part). Suddenly Britain, and the southern and eastern coastlines in particular, appeared to be exposed and defenceless.

Hitler's invasion plan, Operation Sealion, has since been shown to have been wholly inadequate in both scale and preparation. Yet in the summer of 1940 none of this was known. Most people, including those in the armed forces, expected that Hitler would succeed in landing a large force somewhere along the eastern or southern coasts.

The first thrust of Operation Sealion would see attacks against three areas. The XVI Army, 90,000 strong, would capture

including six Panzer divisions, pushing out to take up a line from Portsmouth to the Thames Estuary. The final phase would be the capture of London and the south-east from Essex to Gloucester.[7]

With every prospect of an imminent invasion the fortification of the coast became a priority. Apart from a few guns mounted on the walls of Newhaven Fort there were no modern defences

A 6-inch gun in its emplacement on the ramparts of Newhaven Fort. (By kind permission of Newhaven Fort).

Ramsgate with paratroop regiments securing its flanks from Dover to Pevensey. IX Army, of 40,000 men, was to take West Sussex with paratroopers occupying the coastal fringe from Brighton to Chichester. Finally, the 30,000 troops of VI Army would land at Lyme Bay and move immediately to occupy Bristol.

After consolidating these beachheads, the second stage of the invasion operation would involve a further 260,000 troops,

of any description anywhere along the Sussex shoreline. Everything had to be built from scratch.

Much of the work was undertaken by civil contractors under the supervision of officers of the Royal Engineers. One of the first steps that was taken was the placing of "emergency coast defence batteries" along every part of the threatened coastline.

As so much ordnance had been abandoned in the retreat to

Dunkirk, old 6-inch guns taken from de-commissioned warships were to be used in the emergency batteries.

It was intended that each battery would house two of these guns which were capable of firing armour-piercing shells a distance of seven miles out to sea.

By the end of the second week of June 1940, batteries at Eastbourne, Hastings and Brighton had been completed with others at Bognor Regis, Angmering-on-Sea, Littlehampton, Worthing and Shoreham. The batteries between Brighton and Bognor were manned by No.553 Coast Artillery Regiment, those between Eastbourne and Winchelsea by No.552 Regiment. Newhaven Fort was armed with two 12-pounders and five 6-inch guns, two of which were placed on the ramparts of the fort with the other three on the cliff top immediately to the west. Later in the year further batteries were raised at Cooden Beach, Norman,s Bay and Pevensey.

Fire control headquarters for the Sussex batteries between Bognor Regis and Pevensey Bay was sheltered behind the Downs north of Worthing at Washington, with the guns from Newhaven to Pevensey being under the immediate command of Fortress Control Newhaven. Located in a complex of tunnels cut into the hillside at South Heighton four miles north of Newhaven, Fortress Control was under the authority of the Royal Navy. Commissioned as H.M.S. *Forward*, this underground labyrinth received, processed and distributed maritime intelligence from Fairlight near Hastings through to Bognor Regis. Its importance can be gauged by the fact that from 1942 to 1945 the Commanding Officers at South Heighton held the rank of either Admiral or Vice Admiral. The movement of ships along the coast was monitored by the Chain Home Low radar stations (see Chapter 9) and the information passed through to South Heighton. No gun was allowed to engage an enemy vessel without specific instructions from South Heighton. It had communications links with C-in-C Portsmouth, Vice Admiral Dover, RAF Uxbridge and all the local coastal bases. The tunnels at South Heighton are currently being refurbished with the intention of opening them to the public. [8] The guns along the coast from Hastings eastwards were controlled through Combined Headquarters at Dover Castle.

With the emergency batteries established, more defences were added to almost every stretch of the coast. Rifle-posts, pillboxes, mines, anti-tank barriers and thousands of miles of barbed wire were built, dug and laid along the Sussex shore. Equipment to set the sea on fire with petroleum was installed at Camber Sands, Rye and Church Norton. Amongst the most formidable defensive weapons of 1940 were the Railway Guns. A total of twenty-six of these massive 9.2-inch calibre relics of World War I operated throughout Kent and Sussex on the tracks of the Southern Railway. One of these remarkable weapons was stored at Newington Pit by the side of Glynde Station.

Other defensive measures included the creation of slit trenches for the infantry and sandbag emplacements for heavy machine guns. Roads were blocked with felled trees and, at Worthing, by beach huts filled with shingle. Old vehicles were also placed as obstructions in large fields that might be used as landing grounds by German gliders. Throughout the summer of 1940, military and civil engineers turned these improvised works into a planned and permanent defensive line, some features of which have survived into the twenty-first century.

All road signs and place names were painted out, the great chalk features of the Long Man at Wilmington and the White Horse near Alfriston were grassed over, and the lights of the important port of Newhaven were replicated at Cuckmere Haven to deceive the German bombers. In other parts of the county, dummy airfields were formed and, to further confuse the Luftwaffe, lighting arrays were erected in rural areas to resemble burning towns. [9]

The piers at Bognor Regis, Worthing and Brighton were partially dismantled so that they could not be used as landing jetties by the enemy. Throughout Sussex the beaches were mined and cordoned with barbed wire. Behind this was often a row of concrete anti-tank blocks with pillboxes for rifles or machine guns positioned so as to cover the approach from the beach. The old Royal Military Canal, an obvious defensive feature, once again found a military purpose. The canal and its adjoining road was requisitioned by the War Department in 1935, and in 1940 it was fortified at key points along its length. [10]

Though it was hoped that any enemy landing would be repelled or at least held by these defences, three more lines of defence were constructed further inland. It was recognised that the three major Sussex rivers would, as they have since the Iron Age, play a vital role in the defence of the county. The most important of these stop lines, therefore, ran west to east from the Arun at Bucks Green, through Horsham, Mannings Heath and Handcross to Slaugham near the Ouse, and then down to Newhaven. The backbone of this line was an anti-tank ditch that ran from Warren Wood on the Arun to Slaugham. Every bridge and ford of these two rivers was defended by pillboxes (either anti-tank or anti-infantry) and the bridges or crossings blocked with anti-tank blocks. Infantry trenches, minefields and barbed wire would complete the bridge defences. [11]

The other two stop lines followed the courses of the Arun and the Adur in their passages through the Downs to the sea. The line along the Arun follows the west bank of the river from Littlehampton to Pulborough and along the Adur from Shoreham to Partridge Green and Henfield. Along these two lines the river crossings were covered by concrete 25-pounder field gun emplacements. These lines concluded at the northern end of the Downs as it would have been impossible to prevent the invading forces fanning out across the Weald once they had broken through the hills. Military airfields like Shoreham and Thorney Island were also protected by pillboxes.

Beyond these defences was a vast fortified line protecting London which ran from Scotland, down the eastern side of the country to the Thames estuary and south of the capital to end at the River Severn. Part of this General Headquarters Line - known as Ironside's Line after General Ironside, Commander in Chief Home Forces - travelled from the Medway, through Tonbridge, along the River Uck (parts of which were deepened and widened to increase its effectiveness as a barrier to vehicles), and then

The Battery Observation tower for the Emergency Coastal Battery raised in 1940 at Pett Level. Access to the battery position is through the Pett Level Nature Reserve, (TQ 891135).

followed the line of the Ouse through Lewes to Newhaven. This part of the G.H.Q. Line was supposed to isolate the traditional Sussex and Kent invasion coasts. [12]

General Sir Alan Brooke, who became C.-in-C. Southern Command in July 1940, believed that reliance upon static defensive lines was unsound as such structures could either be penetrated or turned. Instead of placing the defending forces along such lines, the troops were to be massed in strong bodies of mobile reserves which could move against any threatened area. Defensive construction was subsequently limited to fortifying important communications centres (called "nodal" points) throughout Sussex and the south, such as cross-roads and railway junctions. The nodal points were to be held at all costs until the mobile reserves arrived or until the defenders were overwhelmed by the enemy. [13]

By the end of 1941, with the threat of invasion all but vanished, the building programme was gradually wound down. The South-Eastern Command had built more than 3,000 pillboxes and had spent almost £4,000 000 on defensive works. [14]

Though these defences were never tested, other military installations were in frequent combat. These were the anti-aircraft batteries with their accompanying searchlight towers which were sited along the coast, across the Downs, in and around the ports, and other urban areas. Many of these were armed with rapid-firing 40mm Bofor guns - others had heavy 3.7 inch anti-aircraft guns which could fire a 20-pound shell up to 40,000 feet. [15]

The fear of nuclear attack during the Cold War years prompted the RAF to construct a gas and nuclear-proof communications bunker deep within the chalk headland of Beachy Head. Completed in 1953, this huge excavation could accommodate up to 200 personnel. It was abandoned in 1957 and its entrance remains sealed. A similar structure was built at Truleigh Hill, to the north of Shoreham, on the site of the former World War II Chain Home radar station.

Another large bunker complex, to house troops and the South-East Regional Government in the event of a nuclear attack, was built in the Ashdown Forest at Camp Hill. It was completed in 1986 and was still maintained up to 1992. [16]

A type 24 infantry pillbox. The one shown here can be seen near Wadhurst, at the junction of Partridge Lane and the B 2099, (TQ 606336).

A WWII 25-pounder pillbox, located 400 yards north of Bently Bridge, near Henfield, (TQ 197178).

9
Savage Skies
The Battle of Britain

In the spring of 1939 the south of England was once again preparing to withstand an invasion. Following the evacuation of the British Expeditionary Force from Dunkirk in June 1940, it was assumed that the next battle of World War II would be fought on the beaches of southern England. Almost every generation of Sussex men and women had learnt to live with the threat of attack from across the water. This time, though, the threat came not just from the sea but also from the sky and for the first time in history a battle would be fought, and won, almost exclusively in the air.

A successful landing depended upon the Germans achieving air supremacy over both the Channel and the beaches of the south-east. Since the end of the Great War most major powers had been expanding their air arms and developing new aircraft.

The Treaty of Versailles, which had been forced upon a defeated Germany in 1918, banned the Germans from forming an air force. But Russia had allowed the Germans to use a number of their airfields to train pilots and test machines. The Spanish Civil War allowed the Germans to practice their flying skills in a real combat situation. By the outbreak of World War II the German air force, the Luftwaffe, was one of the most powerful weapons in the world but it was organised and equipped for short-range operations in support of the Germans land-based forces, not for a protracted aerial war. [1]

After easy victories against Czechoslovakia, Poland, Belgium and France, in which a combination of aerial bombardment and rapid armoured ground attack - known as the *Blitzkrieg* - had revolutionised warfare, Britain was the only country still in arms against Nazi Germany. All that stood between Hitler and the subjugation of western Europe were the Royal Navy and the fighter squadrons of the Royal Air Force.

In contrast to the expansionist policies in the rest of Europe, Britain scaled down its air force after WWI. By 1922, though the French Armée de l'Air possessed 300 bombers and 300 fighters, the RAF had less than forty aircraft for home defence! It was only in 1936, and only just in time, that ministers authorised an expansion programme that would give Britain an air force capable of defending its shores. This rearmament programme, designed to provide 124 squadrons for home defence, was scheduled for completion on 31 March 1939 - just a few months before Britain would find itself at war with Germany.

On 1 July 1940, Fighter Command, led by Air Chief Marshal Sir Hugh Dowding, could count on only 639 aircraft - having lost more than 450 fighters in the futile battle to save France. Of the former, 545 were front-line Hurricanes and Spitfires the rest were second-rate Blenheims and Defiants. Against this force the Luftwaffe could bring into action 934 Messerschmitt Bf-109 and Bf-110 fighters, 300 Junkers Ju-87 'Stuka' dive-bombers, and 998 Heinkel He-111, Junkers Ju-88 and Dornier Do-17 bombers, plus 157 reconnaissance aircraft - a total of 2,389 aeroplanes [2]. It is hardly surprising that Air Marshal Goering predicted that he would achieve superiority in the skies above Britain in just four days. Yet Britain possessed one great technological advantage over its enemy in the form of radar.

Situated all around the south and east coasts the radar stations, which in Sussex were located at Rye, Fairlight, Pevensey, Beachy Head, Truleigh Hill and Poling, could detect the approach of aircraft up to 120 miles away. Known as the 'Chain Home' range, the network was later supplemented by the 'Chain Home Low' system which was able to detect low-flying aircraft. The numerical superiority enjoyed by the Lufwaffe was considerably reduced by the radar teams' ability to pinpoint German attacks and direct RAF fighters to intercept the enemy bombers before they reached their targets. At the beginning of the Battle of Britain the Germans had not developed radar and they were unable to determine the true purpose of the chain of tall masts along the coast, though they did realise that they were a communications aid of some description and clearly of great importance to the British defensive system.

In addition to the radar stations Sir Hugh Dowding received information from the RAF's "Y" intelligence listening service which intercepted radio-telephone communications from German aircraft. The main listening station was at Cheadle but the first subsidiary station was at Fairlight in Sussex. Of possibly even greater importance was the Government Code and Cipher School at Bletchley Park. Here, with the aid of the Ultra cipher machine, the German Enigma codes were deciphered and their messages interpreted. A great deal of the Luftwaffe's communications were relayed by Enigma and Fighter Command was often aware of the enemy's intentions well in advance - sometimes days in advance - of the actual operation. The final links in the intelligence chain were the posts of the Royal Observer Corps, which was formed in 1925 and was originally manned by two groups of Special Constables covering Kent and Sussex (HQ at Horsham). Each of the 1,400 posts were equipped with a triangulation instrument which gave the observer a positional fix on a grid map. This information, along with the height and number of the "bandits", was sent on to Fighter Command's Operations Rooms.

Fighter Command disposed almost half of its entire force in an arc from Middle Wallop in Hampshire, through Sussex, Kent and Essex to Debden in Suffolk. This area was 11 Group, with its headquarters based at Hillingdon House at Uxbridge in Middlesex. In command of 11 Group was Air Vice Marshal Keith Park. The rest of its force was divided into three other groups. 10 Group covered the south-west; 12 Group the midlands and the east; 13 Group north-east England and Scotland. Each Fighter group was sub-divided into as many as four area "Sectors". Overall strategy was determined by Fighter Command based on the information received through the Operations and Filter rooms at Bently Priory which was at Stanmore in Middlesex. From Bently Priory the battle plan would be passed down to the respective Group or Groups who would then be responsible for control of the battle in their area. The actual tactical handling of the battle would then be taken up by the various Sectors, with each Sector Station possessing its own Operations Room. The system was also highly flexible in that the squadrons could be passed from one sector to another through the network of telephone and teleprinter lines that linked all the Ops Rooms with each other.

The Sector Station for the area between Truleigh Hill above Shoreham to beyond Southhampton was at Tangmere airfield near Chichester. Three squadrons of Hurricanes - Nos. 43, 145 and 601 - were stationed at Tangmere from the end of June until the departure of No.145 Squadron to nearby Westhampnett at the end of July. Though other squadrons would take their place later in the conflict, it was these two units that operated from Tangmere throughout the early, and most critical, days of the battle. The Fighter Interception Unit, flying Blenheims, was also stationed temporarily at Tangmere. The Kent airfields of Kenley and Biggin Hill were responsible for the sectors from Truleigh to Pevensey and Pevensey to Dover respectively. [3]

Officially classified as a satellite of Tangmere, Westhampnett (now known as Goodwood airfield) was a fighter base in its own right. No.145 Squadron, equipped with Hurricanes, was replaced by the Spitfires of No.602 Squadron on 13 August after No.145 Squadron had lost nine planes in the fighting of the previous two days.

Thorney Island airfield was the base for the Blenheim fighter-bombers of Nos. 235, 236 and 59 squadrons. The Blenheims were ineffective in aerial combat but they carried out successful bombing raids against enemy-held installations in France.

Shoreham Airport, though not originally designated as a fighter station, became the home of the Fighter Interception Unit flying Blenheims and Beaufighters when Tangmere came under heavy attack. These aircraft proved to be too heavy for Shoreham's grass runway and the FIU saw little action. The Beaufighters were later joined by a flight of Hurricanes.

Friston, on the Seven Sisters five miles from Eastbourne, was an Emergency Landing Ground for damaged aircraft returning from bombing raids across the Channel. It was later up-graded to a satellite station which first became operational when the Hurricanes of Nos. 253 and 32 Squadrons arrived in June 1942.

They were divided into operational formations known as Geschwaders of around eighty to 100 aeroplanes. Bomber units were Kampfgeshwader, long-range fighter-bomber units were Zerstorergeschwader, the dive-bomber units were Stukageshwader, and Jagdgeschwaders were the fighter units. These units were composed of up to five Gruppen which were

A photograph of the Emergency Coastal Battery at Shoreham in 1940. The battery was located next to the Shoreham Redoubt on Shoreham Beach, (TQ 233045). The searchlight tower can still be seen. (Imperial War Museum, H8226).

Ford airfield near Littlehampton was occupied by the Fleet Air Arm. Designated as H.M.S. *Peregrine*, it was primarily used as a training base for the aircraft carrier squadrons

Across the Channel in Normandy and Brittany the Luftwaffe had been preparing advanced airfields close to the coast throughout the early weeks of the summer of 1940. Telephone and telex systems were installed and fuel dumps established. Luftwaffe Air Fleets, Luftflotte 2 and Luftflotte 3 were to spearhead the attack supported by Luftflotte 5 operating out of Stavanger in Norway. Each of these Air Fleets were large, self-contained battle groups with their own logistical support units.

themselves sub-divided into Staffen which approximated to an RAF squadron. Each Staffen was composed of two or three Schwarm of four aeroplanes each. [4]

Germany did not possess any heavy bombers and in the Battle of Britain it operated four medium to light, twin-engined bombers supported by two types of Messerschmitt fighters. The first of these bombers was the Heinkel He-III. Though its performance was acceptable by the standards of the day, it could only carry 2,134 lbs of bombs with full fuel tanks (compared, for example, with the later British Lancaster bomber which could carry 22,000 lbs). Its 7.9 mm machine guns were manually

The old plaque at Ford airfield when it was the Fleet Air Arm base of H.M.S. Peregrine. The plaque is now in one of the accommodation blocks of H.M.P. Ford, (SU 998027). (By kind permission of the Governor, H.M.P. Ford).

Poling Chain Home radar station of the 1940s. The remains of the radar station are on private agricultural land adjacent to Poling Street, (TQ 045052). (Kind permission Mrs. M. Taylor)

operated and could not easily be brought to bear upon fast-moving targets. The Dornier Do-17 was also inadequately armed and carried an even lighter bomb-load than the Heinkel, though it was a little faster than that bomber.

The two other German bombers were both made by Junkers - the Ju-87 and Ju-88. The Ju-87 was the famous Stuka. It was renowned for its near-vertical bombing dives accompanied by the screaming of its sirens in which it could drop its bombs with great accuracy. It was, however, a slow, ungainly aircraft and it proved to be an easy target for the pilots of the Royal Air Force Fighter Command. The Ju-88 was by far the Luftwaffe's finest bomber. It could deliver its pay-load either horizontally or in a Stuka-like dive. For a bomber it was very fast, being only thirty miles per hour slower than a Hurricane's operational fighting speed and it could out-perform a Bristol Blenheim fighter.

The Messerschmitt Bf-109 was a single-seat, high-performance interceptor fighter. It was faster than either the Hurricane or the Spitfire and it was more heavily armed. Whilst the Bf-109 was regarded as being less manoeuvrable than its two main British fighters it did have one great advantage over its rivals in a dog-fight. Because of its fuel injection system the Luftwaffe pilots could escape from trouble by pushing the Messerschmitt into a direct nose-dive.

The British planes, with simple float carburettors, had to be thrown into a half-roll to swill petrol into their engines to prevent stalling before they could dive. Those few seconds, won or lost, could prove decisive. The Bf-109, however, was designed as an interceptor, not as a bomber escort, and it could not carry sufficient fuel to operate for long periods of time over England.

Goering's much-vaunted "Destroyer", the Bf-110, was a much larger, twin-engined aircraft. It had a very impressive armament with its four machine guns and two 20mm cannon in the nose and another gun operated by a rear-gunner. It was also a very fast aircraft for its day. Yet the Bf-110 suffered from one major defect which greatly reduced its effectiveness - it was structurally weak in the tail assembly.

To oppose these aircraft the RAF had the Hawker Hurricane and the superb Supermarine Spitfire. Both were capable of speeds considerably in excess of 300 miles per hour. They proved to be extremely manoeuvrable and they were armed with eight Vickers-Browning machine guns situated in the wings. These were specialist interceptor fighters, designed for aerial combat. Though Fighter Command possessed far fewer aircraft than the Luftwaffe, the vast majority of the machines sent across the Channel by the Germans were bombers. The air war over southern England, particularly in the first weeks of the conflict, was predominately a conflict between German bombers and British fighters. Dowding's pilots were specifically instructed to avoid confrontations with enemy fighters and instead to concentrate their efforts, whenever practical, upon the bombers. It is this simple fact that explains the result of the Battle of Britain. In addition to the Hurricane and Spitfire, Fighter Command operated the sluggish fighter variant of the Bristol Blenheim and the out-dated Boulton-Paul Defiant.

Tactically the opposing air forces adopted very different formations at the start of the war. Each RAF squadron of twelve planes was divided into four sections of three. These 'flights' flew very close together in either "V" or line astern formations as a section of three or along with other sections of the squadron. When an enemy was located the fighters would peel away one after another, firing short bursts as they dived past the opposing aircraft. By contrast the German fighters used the Schwarm formation, which the British pilots called the 'finger-four'. Developed during the Spanish Civil War, the Schwarm involved two pairs of widely spread aircraft each flying at different heights and in staggered positions. The superiority of the Schwarm soon became apparent and the British pilots eventually abandoned their close order flying and embraced the principles of fighting in pairs in looser formations. [5]

The Luftwaffe had been flying reconnaissance and combat patrols across the Channel since June. British ships had been sunk and aircraft on both sides had been shot down. Most of these raids were at night with fourteen ports, sixteen industrial plants and thirteen airfields becoming targets. The Luftwaffe achieved little in strategic terms during this period and it gave the RAF time to build up its fighter aircraft strength. Hundreds of Spitfires and Hurricanes were being turned out of the factories which, on 14 May, had come under the authority of Lord Beaverbrook. As Minister of Aircraft Production, Beaverbrook re-organised production schedules and concentrated the work upon building and repairing fighters, leaving only limited capacity for other aircraft. The result was a doubling of fighter production to almost 500 aircraft a month by September.

In July the attacks intensified with 10 July now being considered the first day of the Battle of Britain. On that day the target selected by the Luftwaffe was a convoy of ships passing through the Dover straits. The Home Chain system detected an unusually large number of aircraft in the sky above Calais. Park waited cautiously. If this was the start of the anticipated invasion he had to deploy his slender resources carefully. When it became apparent that the Germans were only attacking the convoy, Park despatched just twenty-six fighters to help the ships.

Against some seventy Do-17s, Me Bf-109s and 110s, the Hurricanes and Spitfires claimed four kills for the loss of three of their own fighters. [6]

The following day -11 July - a large formation of Stukas escorted by Bf-110s flew along the Sussex coast heading for Portland. Tangmere's No.601 Squadron were sent to intercept. Diving out of the sun the Hurricanes broke the formation, claiming two Ju87s. Later that day No.601 were again in action, this time as the Heinkels of Kampfgeschwader 55 attacked Portsmouth. No.145 Squadron was also scrambled, catching the German bombers as they headed for home across the Channel. The raid had cost the Luftwaffe dearly. The German air force lost twenty-five planes, having dropped just 168 bombs.

Successful attacks against British shipping, including Royal Navy destroyers, had stopped almost all traffic through the Channel. Yet Dowding and Park were using their fighter squadrons only sparingly, knowing that the big battles for mastery of the skies over Britain were still to come.

Over the course of the next month the Tangmere squadrons were in frequent action over the Kent, Sussex and Hampshire coasts and along the Channel as the Luftwaffe attempted to weaken Fighter Command in preparation for the great series of raids that Hitler hoped would drive Britain to the negotiating table. During this "softening-up" period, which was named *Kanalkampf* by the Germans, Bf-109s prowled along the coastline and attacked allied shipping hoping to draw the British fighters into action. These tactics resulted in the destruction of 117 British fighters - one sixth of Fighter Commands original strength - by the end of July. The battle had scarcely begun and, though the Luftwaffe lost considerably more aircraft during this period. Dowding could ill afford such losses. Fortunately for the RAF the responsibility for the next phase of the battle was handed over to the German bombers and they would prove to be less formidable opponents than the Messerschmitts. It was at this time, just two weeks before the crucial weeks of the conflict, that Westhampnett airfield became fully operational with the transfer of No. 145 Squadron from Tangmere.

Another convoy attempted to slip through the Channel on 8 August. This time the twenty-five merchant ships were escorted by anti-aircraft destroyers and barrage balloon vessels. As the convoy crept past Dover, German torpedo-armed E-boats raced from their bases in Northern France and sunk three of the ships and, as it approached the Isle of Wight, the Luftwaffe swept in for the kill. A formation of more than eighty Stukas from Stukageschwaders 1, 2 and 27, twice bombed the convoy before eleven squadrons from 10 and 11 Groups, including Westhampnett's No.145 squadron could intervene. Three Stukas were shot down but a further four ships were sunk and others were damaged.

In the afternoon the Stukas returned to the attack. Again No.145 Squadron, as well as Tangmere's No.43 Squadron, was scrambled. The Ju-87s were escorted by a large body of Bf-109s and a major air battle took place over the Isle of Wight. By the end of the day's action the Germans had lost twenty-seven aircraft with No.43 Squadron losing six and No.145 Squadron five, (including the Hurricane of Squadron Leader John Peel).

Peel was later rescued from the sea near Bolougne. Only four ships of the ill-fated convoy reached Swanage harbour. No. 145 Squadron had been the most successful squadron that day with two pilots able to claim three enemy aircraft and one pilot, Flight Lieutenant Roy Dutton, having five "kills" to his credit. A congratulatory visit to Westhampnett by Dowding, accompanied by the Secretary of State for Air and the Chief of the Air Staff, was later followed by a visit from the Duke of Gloucester.

On the 11th and 12th the Tangmere and Westhampnett Hurricanes were again in action, defending Portland and Portsmouth from large-scale attacks by Junkers 88s and Heinkels supported by Bf-109s and 110s. Again No.145 Squadron suffered heavy casualties, losing eight aircraft in the two days of fighting. The Hurricanes were joined by the Spitfires of No.266 Squadron which arrived at Tangmere on 9 August. Though this unit only stayed for three days it was involved in the battle of 12 August and lost two of its Spitfires.

The Luftwaffe's operation to destroy the RAF was labelled *Adlerangriff* or Eagle Attack, the first stage of which was to be the demolition of the radar network. And so early on 12 August, Junkers and Dorniers bombed the radar stations from Dover to the Isle of Wight. Rye radar station was severely damaged but a back-up power supply brought the equipment back on line by lunch time. Pevensey's power main was also hit but the station was able to remain on air. A number of the coastal airfields were also attacked on this day. The result of the first day of *Adlerangriff* was the loss of twenty-two British fighters whilst the Luftwaffe suffered thirty-one aircraft casualties. Importantly the radar network had not been disabled. Day two - *Alder Tag* or Eagle Day - was to be the day that the Fighter Command's airfields were destroyed. It too would be a failure.

On the morning of 13 August a bank of low cloud hung over the Channel and the Luftwaffe's operations had to be postponed until late in the afternoon. Earlier, around midday, the scheduled attack by the Heinkels and Junkers 88s of Kampfgruppe 54 had been cancelled but the fighter escort of twenty Bf-110s had not been informed of the cancellation and they, alone, continued their mission against the naval base at Portland. They were met by a number of RAF squadrons including No.601 from Tangmere. In the ensuing encounter KG 54 lost five 110s, No.601 four Hurricanes. Similar confusion led to seventy-four Dorniers of KG 2, which were already airborne, to continue on to their target although their escort of Bf-110s had been ordered back to base. The Dorniers, however, reached their objective and severely damaged the Coastal Command station at Eastchurch.

The main raids of Eagle Day came in the afternoon. Both Tangmere squadrons were scrambled to defend the docks and installations of Portland and Southampton. Waves of Ju-87s, escorted by Bf-109s and 110s, broke through the British fighters to hit Southampton and Andover. Attacks against the Kent airfields by massed Stuka Staffel were also delivered with Detling airfield near Maidstone being badly damaged. By the end of the day the Luftwaffe had flown 1,485 sorties to the RAF's 700 with the Germans losing forty-five planes compared with just thirteen of the RAF, of which three were from Tangmere's No.43 Squadron.

Day three of *Adlerangriff* was far less intense. Limited raids and reconnaissance patrols resulted in nineteen German aircraft being lost against only eight British machines. Middle Wallop was the only airfield to be attacked.

Clear skies on 15 August heralded the Luftwaffe's greatest effort of the conflict. It was to be a huge operation with all three Luftflotten attacking the British coast from the Firth of Forth to the West Country.

In the first air raid of the day over Sussex, Stukas knocked out Rye radar station with a direct hit. This was followed by a massive attack against the Portsmouth and Southampton area and No. 43 Squadron was scrambled to intercept the enemy over the Isle of Wight. Moments later a large formation of Ju-87s from Stukageschwader 2 dived out of the bright midday sun above Tangmere. The Stukas screamed down and released their bombs across the exposed airfield. The runway was bombed, one of the hangars was hit as were parts of the accommodation blocks. Five

Blenheims of the Fighter Interception Unit and a Hurricane of No.43 Squadron were damaged on the ground before the rest of the squadron turned back to defend their base. The Stuka was no match for the Hurricane and nine German planes were shot down with three others damaged. Only one of Tangmere's Hurricanes was lost and three damaged

A painting of the Control Tower at Tangmere airfield. The tower can still be seen to the north of the old airfield at the end of a road which runs besides the present-day aviation museum, (SU 9136066).

The Kent airfields endured similar attacks and an engine factory at Rochester and the Short Brothers factory, where the Stirling bomber was in production, were severely damaged. Two factories at Croydon were also hit - these were the first bombs to land in the London suburbs. Luftflotten 5 also attacked the north-east from its base at Stavanger in the mistaken belief that some of 13 Group's squadrons had been sent to the south to help 11 Group. The attack was a disaster for Luftflotte 5 which lost sixteen of its total of 123 bombers and seven of its thirty-four fighters. By the end of this crucial day the RAF had flown 974 sorties and had shot seventy-five German planes out of the sky.

On the following day, 16 August, the Luftwaffe concentrated their forces upon the airfields of Kent, Hampshire and Sussex. Again Stukas headed in the direction of Tangmere escorted by Bf-109s. Skipping passed the bomb craters in the grass runway both squadrons of Hurricanes took to the air but they could not prevent some of the dive-bombers reaching the airfield. The six remaining Blenheims of the FIU were destroyed on the ground, along with seven Hurricanes and one Magistar trainer. Pilot Officer William Fisk of No.601 Squadron successfully landed his damaged Hurricane only to be strafed by the Germans whilst he was still in the cockpit. He died two days later. Fisk was an American volunteer and he was the first American to be killed in action in the air war over Britain. Five hangars were struck, two of which were completely wrecked. The workshops, pump-house, stores and sick bay were hit. An air-raid shelter was smashed and the station's power, communications, water and sanitation systems were severed. Over forty vehicles were damaged with thirteen personnel killed and another twenty wounded. Tangmere's Hurricanes drove off the attackers, shooting down four bombers but losing four aircraft of their own. [7]

Other dog-fights had broken out all over Sussex. A Heinkel 111 of Kampfgeshwader 55 was hit by RAF fighters over Brighton, the machine crashing to earth on the Downs above High Salvington. The tail-plane of Oberleutenant Ernst Hollekamp's Bf-110 was shot away over Eastbourne and the aircraft broke apart in mid-air. Hollekamp's rear gunner baled out as the machine began to disintegrate but Hollekamp went down with his plane, the wreckage of which was scattered across three-quarters of a mile of Sussex countryside. His body was recovered from the roof of a house in Gaudlick Road in Eastbourne. [8]

The Spitfires of Westhampnett's No.602 Squadron also took to the air in defence of Tangmere. Two Spitfires were damaged but both returned to the airfield. Later in the afternoon No.602 scrambled again, this time claiming two Messerschmitt 110s of ZG 76 operating from the Norwegian coast. Gosport, West Malling, Manston, Lee-on-Solent, and Farnborough airfields were all bombed. At Brize Norton, Ju-88s destroyed forty-six aircraft on the ground, including a number of Hurricanes. Ventnor Chain Home station was again hit and put out of service.

After two days of heavy attacks the main fighter base in Sussex was in a terrible state. Sector Operations was moved to a school in Chichester and what little remained of the Fighter Interceptor Unit was transferred to Shoreham airfield. Fortunately for Tangmere the Luftwaffe spent most of 17 August in reconnaissance missions in an attempt to evaluate the extent of the devastation that they had inflicted over the previous days. This allowed the personnel at Tangmere to make a start on repairs to the airfield and its installations. [9]

The Luftwaffe estimated that Fighter Command had only 300 serviceable aircraft left and that another intense series of raids on the airfields on 18 August would see the end of the RAF as an effective defensive force. In fact Fighter Command had almost twice that many planes, though it was desperately short of pilots.

Goering's first raids of 18 August were against the Kent airfields. Nine Dorniers from KG 76 flew low over Beachy Head and followed the Brighton to London railway to attack Kenley. The Dorniers had been spotted by the Observer Corps and Kenley's Hurricanes were waiting for the German bombers. Only one Dornier returned intact to its base. Biggin Hill was attacked and damaged in a raid by sixty Heinkel He-111s.

It was not until 14:00 hours that Stukas bombed the Chain Home station at Poling. Some ninety bombs were dropped around the radar installation which was very seriously damaged. This success cost the Luftwaffe dearly. At the approach of the Stukas, Nos. 43, 601 and Westhampnett's No.602 Squadron were all scrambled and no less than twelve of the Junkers 87s were shot down.

A second wing of Stukas from SG 77, escorted by Bf-109s from JG 27, then attacked along the coast. Due to faulty intelligence the Fleet Air Arm bases at Thorney Island and Ford had been classified as fighter bases and it was upon these two airfields that twenty-eight bombers unleashed their deadly cargoes.

With just six Lewis machine guns to defend the entire airfield the Stuka pilots could pick their targets at will. Ford airfield was destroyed in less than 10 minutes. Thirty-nine aircraft were damaged and many installations smashed including the armoury. The fuel dump was also hit, setting it on fire and a dense black cloud engulfed the airfield. Over 100 people were killed or wounded. Ford was so severely damaged that it was abandoned by the Fleet Air Arm and their remaining aircraft were transferred to other sites. [10]

The Luftwaffe's other objective was Thorney Island. This time the Stukas met some resistance as a number of Thorney Island's Blenheims of No. 235 Squadron managed to get airborne before the Junkers began their fearsome screeching dives. Two hangars were wrecked (along with the three Avro Ansons inside them), and a fuel dump was hit which ignited with a massive explosion.

As the Stukas circled over the island, No.235 Squadron's Blenheims were joined by the Hurricanes and Spitfires of Nos. 43, 601 and 602 Squadrons. Ten Stukas were brought down over Thorney Island with a further three over Ford.

Stukas were never again used against Britain. Though they could bomb with great accuracy they were far slower than the British fighters. Even No.235 Squadron's lumbering Blenheims shot down two Ju-87s over Thorney Island. The Stukas were valued and effective bombers and Goering dare not lose any more in air-to-air combat for which they were clearly unsuited. The Reichsmarschall also changed tactics, and from 19 August the individual Kampfgeschwaden were allowed to select their own targets. The German aircrews were informed that Fighter Command could not defend Britain for much longer. A few more days of intense endeavour, they were told, would see the Luftwaffe as masters of the sky. But the battered airfields, many of which German intelligence believed had been put out of action, were quickly patched up and continued to be operational. Also, where possible, Dowding rotated his tired squadrons to quieter sectors for a few days rest.

Apart from a few isolated raids the Luftwaffe was kept grounded for the next four days by poor weather. But on Saturday 24 August the onslaught was renewed with raids against Manston, Hornchurch and Portsmouth. Luftflotten 3 switched to night attacks with the London suburbs being bombed extensively for the first time in the war. Casualties for the day amounted to thirty-eight German and twenty-two British aircraft.

Late in the afternoon of the 26th German bombers were detected as they approached Portsmouth. No.43 Squadron was scrambled and engaged the enemy formation over the city. The attackers were driven off at a heavy cost as No.43 Squadron lost six planes, though all the pilots survived. Such losses were repeated across the south-east and Goering's claims that the RAF was nearing defeat were far from exaggerated. Between 8 and 18 August ninety-four of Fighter Command's pilots had been posted killed or missing and the raw recruits that took their place were no match for the Luftwaffe's veterans. The Stukas had been easy meat for the Spitfires and Hurricanes but the Heinkels and Dorniers in their tight formations protected by the fast Bf-109s were a different proposition.

Night raids by Luftflotte 3 intensified on the 27th with attacks against airfields and factories across the south and east from Portsmouth to Lincolnshire. By operating at night the Luftwaffe's losses were reduced to single figures but so were those of the RAF. If Germany was to invade England the air battle had to be won and this could only be achieved by destroying Fighter Command. This could not be accomplished by night attacks alone. So for the next twelve days the Luftwaffe hammered the airfields of the south and east. Each time they were met by Fighter Command. Each time, by sheer weight of numbers, they broke through to their targets. It was a battle of attrition, and the side that suffered the heaviest casualties would lose. Confirmed kills were meticulously logged on both sides and the totals analysed. Thus on 28 August the Luftwaffe lost thirty-one aircraft to the RAF's twenty-eight; on 29 August the score was seventeen to nine. The statistics, however, hid an important fact. Every time a German aeroplane was shot down over England the crew would either be killed or captured, whereas many English pilots in the same situation were able to parachute to, or crash land in, safety. Thus on 31 August, for instance, the Luftwaffe lost forty-one aircraft and the RAF thirty-nine, and though these were the heaviest losses incurred by Fighter Command in a single day, only fourteen of its pilots were killed.

On the 28th a small two-seater German Gotha 145 biplane set off from France with mail for the troops occupying Jersey. In poor visibility the pilot lost his way and flew over the Sussex coast. The aircraft was spotted by the Observer Corps and two fighters were sent to intercept. The Gotha was forced to land near Lewes racecourse and the pilot was taken to Lewes police station. The captured mail provided military intelligence with some useful information. The Gotha, meanwhile, was taken by the RAF, re-painted, and subsequently used in a communications role. [11]

Sussex was not seriously attacked again until 30 August, when a large force, including Heinkel-111s, closed in upon Shoreham and Tangmere. No.601 Squadron had been stood down for a period of well-earned rest and No.17 Squadron had temporarily taken its place. When the German bombers appeared over Tangmere Nos. 43 and 17 squadrons were in the air defending the Kent airfields and Tangmere was unprotected.

The airfield took another terrible pounding. At the same time Pevensey, Rye and Beachy Head Chain Home stations, along with three others in Kent, were blacked out when there power supplies was severed. No.43 Squadron also lost their Squdaron Leader, "Tubby" Badger, who was shot down over Kent. The Luftwaffe continued to concentrate its efforts against the Kent airfields and over the next few days the staff at Tangmere were able to repair much of the damage inflicted upon the buildings and installations.

On 1 September Goering ordered the night attacks to be directed upon Britain's aircraft industry. Despite mounting losses, Britain's war production was gaining pace and it was able to replace its lost aircraft. The next day, 2 September, Hitler ordered yet another change in strategy. Instead of directing the main strength of the Luftwaffe against the airfields of the RAF, the principal target was to be London. It was argued that the RAF would have no choice but to defend London and it would be over the skies of the capital that Fighter Command would finally be destroyed. This was one of the most significant decisions of World War II. Though there is no doubt that the RAF suffered major casualties during the "Blitz" of London, the fighter bases were given a reprieve at a time when they were on the verge of collapse.

The date set for the start of the Blitz was 7 September. In the days leading up to this date the Luftwaffe continued to pound the airfields and aircraft factories. Between 2 September and 6 September the Luftwaffe hit eight airfields and the Thameshaven oil tanks. The Vickers factory, where the Wellington bomber was being built, was bombed, injuring some 600 workers and killing a further eighty-four people. During this short period of time the Germans also shot down 107 British aircraft. If the Luftwaffe had continued to attack the aircraft factories and Fighter Command's airfields in the south, it is quite possible that they could eventually have achieved their aim of air supremacy over southern England and the Channel.

London was within a few minutes flying time of 12 Group's southern-most airfields. Having spent weeks in comparative idleness whilst 11 Group bore the brunt of the fighting, Leigh-Mallory's men could at last play an effective part in the battle. Three days earlier, on 30 August, 12 Group's No.242 Squadron, led by Squadron Leader Douglas Bader, had been scrambled to intercept a large formation of German raiders to the north of London. Bader achieved a degree of success against the Germans but he was angered by seeing so many enemy aircraft escape unhurt. He later argued, and argued successfully, that if he had led more than just one squadron of twelve 'planes he would have inflicted far heavier casualties. His reasoning led to the introduction of the famous "Big Wing". Bader was given command over three squadrons of Hurricanes and two of Spitfires - a maximum of sixty aircraft.

The final phase of the Battle of Britain began on 7 September. Throughout the day and night the Heinkels, Dorniers and Junkers 88s ravaged London. During daylight hours the Hurricanes and Spitfires, and during the night the Defiants, flew sortie after sortie. Losses on both sides were immense. The destiny, not only of Britain, but also of Europe, hung in the balance. Little wonder that Churchill declared "Never in the field of human conflict was so much owed by so many to so few".

The battle that raged over London saw No.43 Squadron lose another Hurricane before it was at last relieved by No.213 Squadron. Tangmere was now the station for Nos. 213 and 607 squadrons, the latter losing seven Hurricanes during the first days of the Blitz.

It is difficult to estimate just how closely Hitler came to destroying Fighter Command. His decision to attack civilian targets was certainly wrong. Not only did it stiffen Britain's resolve but it also resulted in reprisals against Berlin. Officially, Battle of Britain Day is celebrated on 15 September though the air war over Britain continued for another two months. Realistically, it ended on 7 September when Hitler directed the Luftwaffe to exclude the airfields of Fighter Command from their list of objectives.

Apart from the relief given to the fighter stations, Goering's plan possessed another serious flaw. Whilst the principle of compelling the RAF to put every available plane into the air to defend the capital was sound the Reichmarshal overlooked the fact that London was on the very edge of the Bf-109s' effective range. In raids against the coastal airfields the Messerschmitts could provide the German bombers with protection all the way to their targets, engage the RAF fighters that tried to attack them, and still have enough fuel left to escort the bombers back across the Channel. By the time that the German formations reached London, however, the 109s had only a few minutes air time over the capital before they were obliged to return home. This left the bombers of the Luftwaffe fatally vulnerable. [12]

Dowding was also facing difficulties. During August over 300 fighter pilots had been killed or were seriously wounded, whereas the operational training units had turned out only 260 replacement pilots in the same period. These raw recruits were easy targets for the experienced Luftwaffe fliers and many became victims themselves within days of joining their squadrons. No.603 Squadron, for example, flew into Hornchurch on 28 August and just eight days later it was withdrawn after losing sixteen aircraft and twelve pilots.

The first great raid on London began in the afternoon of 7 September, when more than 300 bombers and 600 fighters headed directly for the capital, followed that night by another 247 German aircraft. The next day Stukas attacked a large British convoy of ships that was attempting to pass through the Channel. The convoy, which had already been attacked by

German E-boats, lost a number of ships before the Ju-87s were intercepted by Hurricanes from Westhampnett's No.145 Squadron and Tangmere's No.43 Squadron. As usual, when Stukas met British fighters they were severely mauled, but the escorting German Messerschmitts shot down six of the Sussex-based Hurricanes.

Night attacks against London continued with Liverpool also being added to the Luftwaffe's target list. The Luftwaffe's daily losses had reduced significantly due to the virtual abandonment of large daylight operations. Total losses for the 12th, 13th and 14th of September amounted to just thirty aircraft and this led to the belief at Luftwaffe headquarters that Fighter Command was in disarray. So, on 15 September, the German air force mounted huge raids in the morning and afternoon. Both attacks were broken up by the British fighters, with the enemy losing sixty aircraft - the heaviest casualty figures since 18 August. The Luftwaffe was stunned at the RAF's continuing ability to resist and it was clear that Fighter Command was far from beaten.

The following day Goering held a meeting with his senior Luftflotten commanders. In an attempt to reduce the scale of losses he demanded that they decreased the size of the bomber formations and increased their fighter escorts. Massive raids, such as those of the previous day, would not be undertaken again unless weather conditions were perfect and adequate fighter cover was available.

On the 17th Hitler postponed the invasion of England for an indefinite period. His thoughts now turned to his attack upon Russia and the invasion forces along the Channel coast were gradually withdrawn. None of this was yet known in Britain as the nightly raids continued unabated. The most damaging attacks were delivered on 25 and 26 September, when the Bristol Aeroplane Company's works were bombed and the important Spitfire factory at Southampton was completely demolished. The final, large-scale, daylight raid over Britain took place on the last day of September. It cost the Lufwaffe more than forty aircraft.

Park also announced a change in tactics. The Me Bf-109s had

proven more than a match for the Hurricanes but the slightly faster and more manoeuvrable Spifires had been successful against the German fighters. The British fighters were now regularly flying in Wings of two or three squadrons composed of the same type of aircraft, so Park ordered his Hurricane wings to concentrate on the bombers whilst the Spitfires engaged the fighters.

Park's new tactics soon became redundant as from the beginning of October the German bombers were used almost exclusively for night-time operations. But Goering wanted to maintain pressure against Fighter Command and he attempted to combine the speed of his Messerschmitt fighters with the destructive power of the bombers by converting some 250 Bf-109s and 110s to fighter-bombers. The 109s were loaded with a single 250kg bomb and the 110s with up to 700kgs of ordnance.

The first fighter-bomber raid was mounted on 1 October against Kent, Portsmouth and Southhampton. The fighter-bomber formations, escorted by Me Bf-109s which had not been converted into bombers, flew at high altitude (around 20,000 feet). This made them difficult to plot and meant a long, hard climb for the Spitfires and Hurricanes in which they were vulnerable to counter-attacks from above by the Messerschmitts. The consequence was that for the first time RAF daily losses exceeded those of the Luftwaffe on a number of occasions during the month of October. The raids, however, were not a huge success. As soon as they were intercepted by the RAF, the pilots of the fighter-bombers jettisoned their bomb load whether they were over their designated target or not. Park also ordered readiness squadrons to patrol the skies above the sector stations at between 20,000 and 25,000 feet so that they could engage the enemy on equal terms.

With autumn approaching and the nights drawing in, the last days of October signalled the end of any invasion threat for that year. The Battle of Britain had cost the RAF 915 aeroplanes and the Luftwaffe a staggering 1,733 aircraft. The nightly bombing raids upon industrial centres, docks and cities did not end, however, and to combat this a number of Hurricanes and Spitfire squadrons, including Westhampnett's No.602 Squadron, were temporarily switched to night-flying. The RAF also began to deploy the first purpose-built night-fighters. The Bristol Beaufighters of No.219 Squadron flew into Tangmere on 12 October. Equipped with the recently developed Airborne Interception Radar these fast and powerfully armed fighters were able to locate the enemy's bombers in conjunction with the ground-based radar stations. Ford aerodrome, which had been rebuilt after the heavy punishment it had received in August, was taken over by the RAF and incorporated into No.11 Group Fighter Command, flying the Mark IF Blenheims of No.23 Squadron which were specifically adapted for night interception roles.

With few daylight duties to occupy the Spitfire and Hurricane squadrons these aircraft turned increasingly to the offensive. At Tangmere the Spitfires of Nos. 616 and 145 squadrons undertook attacking patrols, known as "Rodeos" into northern France. With no radar network to warn the Germans of their approach the fighters were able to steal upon the Luftwaffe's forward airfields and catch the enemy aircraft sitting impotently upon the ground.

Though limited and opportunistic, these raids marked the turning point in the war. The RAF was no longer restricted solely to the defensive. The Battle of Britain was over. The Battle for Europe was about to begin.

Between the outbreak of hostilities and the end of 1940, some 180 German and 120 British planes were shot down over Sussex and the seas around its coastline. These incidents claimed the lives of 61 British and 143 German airmen with a further 147 Germans captured and taken prisoner. 310 civilians were also killed in Sussex throughout 1940 as a result of enemy action. [13]

10
Dieppe to D-Day
The Last Battles

Almost as soon as the British Expeditionary Force had been driven from the beaches of Dunkirk, Churchill had been determined to return to Europe in triumph. It would be many years before Britain could build its military strength to a level capable of challenging Hitler's hold upon the Continent, but meanwhile Britain would not remain cowering on the defensive. The RAF had proven itself against the Germans in the air and it was the RAF that would carry the war into occupied Europe and, ultimately, into the very heart of the Reich.

Leigh-Mallory, who had taken over from Hugh Dowding at the head of Fighter Command, was a proponent of the "Non-stop Offensive" and the airfields of the south were in action over France, and later Belgium and Holland, almost every day. However, Leigh-Mallory's men could not be employed exclusively in missions across the Channel. The Luftwaffe continued its night-time attacks against the major British cities and ports and Fighter Command was frequently deployed in defensive roles and escorts for shipping in the Channel. As well as attacks from the air, Sussex also suffered raids from the sea, including an incident in January 1941 when two German E-boats cruised along the Sussex coast firing at troops working on the beaches and another in 1942 when a German submarine sailed up the Cuckmere River and fired several shots at the Exceat Bridge.

Some of the offensive flights over France towards the end of 1940 were patrols undertaken by single fighters or flights of up to six aircraft. The aim of these patrols was to "attack and destroy enemy aircraft, or, if impractical, suitable ground military objectives." [1] Known by the code name "Rhubarb" these raids proved to be of limited value and they were soon overtaken by operations by Wings of two or three squadrons. In March 1941, Squadron Leader Douglas Bader was offered command of one of these wings with the rank of Wing Commander (Flying), his objective being offensive action against German targets across the Channel. He was given the choice of operating from either Biggin Hill in Kent or Tangmere in Sussex. He chose Tangmere. Under his command were three squadrons of Spitfires based at Westhampnett and Merston.

It was expected that these larger formations would tempt the German fighters into the air but as the Spitfires and Hurricanes could do little harm to the Luftwaffe on the ground, the Germans simply ignored these patrols. Soon the fighters were accompanied by a few Blenheim or Stirling bombers which the Luftwaffe could not ignore. Their effectiveness, however, remained marginal and Allied losses in the missions were comparatively heavy. These operations bore the code name "Circus". In order to deceive the Germans and convince them that the eventual re-invasion of Europe would take place in the Pas de Calais, twice as many missions were flown into that area than into other parts of France.

Fighter Command was primarily organised and equipped as a defensive weapon. The offensive into Europe demanded a change in both structure and equipment. Towards the end of 1943 Fighter Command became the Second Tactical Air Force and a bomber group was added to the existing fighter wings. Leigh-Mallory remained its commander. The aircraft available to the opposing air forces had changed considerably since the Battle of Britain. In September 1941, the Luftwaffe introduced the Focke Wulf 190 fighter. It was faster than the Spitfire, could reach 26,000 feet in twelve minutes - with an operational ceiling of almost 35,000 feet - and it was highly manoeuvrable. Improved versions of the Messerschmit Bf-109s were also introduced.

The RAF had also received a new aircraft, the Hawker Typhoon. Though very fast at low and medium altitudes, it soon proved to be no match for the FW 190s and the later versions of the Bf-109s in aerial combat. It's speed and it's powerful armament (which included rockets) made it highly effective as a fighter-bomber and in close support roles for ground troops. The American Mustang, many powered by Rolls Royce Merlin engines, was the United States Air Force's principle fighter and a number of RAF squadrons were also equipped with this aeroplane. The Mustang was considered to be the best fighter plane of WWII. The Hurricane was no longer regarded as a front-line fighter but the Spitfire had continued to be developed and the majority of the Leigh-Mallory's squadrons were equipped with the most recent Sptifire marks.

During this time Tangmere had an additional role. It was from there that many secret agents of the Special Operations Executive were flown into France. The agents were housed at nearby Bignor Manor which operated under the guise of a convalescent home for wounded officers. Under conditions of the utmost secrecy the agents were taken from the manor and flown across the Channel at night, usually in Lysanders which were painted black and were without identification markings. [2]

One of the most important pre-requisites for a successful re-invasion of Europe (which was code named Operation Overlord) would be the establishment and maintenance of air superiority over the landing beaches and the enemy's interior lines of communication. In order to help achieve the former, attacks were to be delivered against industrial units associated with aircraft construction and against the German fighters, both on the ground and in the air. Of the latter, railway stations became prime targets and this was later extended to include all trains and railway installations. In all of these operations the Sussex airfields were to play a key role.

In preparation for this a number of temporary airfields, known as Advanced Landing Grounds, were formed in the south. They were built to a common specification, with each having two metal runways, both fifty yards wide, the principle one being 1,600 yards long and the other 1,400 yards. In conformance with their temporary status no permanent buildings were erected. At each ALG a maximum of four Blister hangars were raised with all personnel being accommodated in tents or local houses.

Funtington, to the north-west of Chichester, was the most westerly of the Sussex ALGs. It became operational in February 1943 with two squadrons of Mustangs. These squadrons, Nos. 4 and 268, flew reconnaissance and deep penetration flights into enemy territory to strike at any available targets. Known as "Ranger" patrols, they were part of the "softening up" process, putting a strain on German resources and under-mining morale.

The following year hard standings were laid and in August 1944 three squadrons of Typhoon IBs replaced the old Mark I Mustangs. These three Canadian squadrons (Nos. 428, 439 and 440) were tasked to attack V1 rocket sites in Northern France and the Typhoons, in their fighter-bomber role proved effective against such comparatively small targets. After just three weeks at Funtington another Canadian unit, 144 Wing, flying Spitfire IXBs, took their place. Led by the man who was to become the Allies top ace with thirty-eight accredited kills, "Johnny" Johnson, Nos. 441, 442 and 443 squadrons escorted bombing raids in the build up to the date of the re-invasion - D-Day. [3]

To the east of Funtington, and a mile or so to the south of Chichester, an ALG was laid at Apuldram. Completed by the end of May 1943, it was firstly the home of 124 Wing with three squadrons of Typhoons. The Typhoons flew sorties against enemy airfields and later against radar stations until 1 July, when the airfield was mothballed until the intensification of aerial operations preceding D-Day. [4]

A further four miles south of Chichester, between the village of Church Norton and Selsey, an ALG was built which became operational in May 1943. 121 Wing, consisting of No.65 Squadron, flying Spitfires, and No. 245 with Typhoons, was based at Selsey until July when the airfield, like many of the ALGs, was closed down to allow improvements to be made in preparation for Operation Overlord. [5]

Bognor ALG opened in June 1943, when 122 Wing with Nos.

19, 122 and 602 squadrons of Spitfires arrived and were tasked for ground attack missions. After just a month of such operations the Spitfires left Bognor and the airfield was not used again until March 1944. During this dormant period the airfield was provided with Blister hangars and hardstanding. [6]

Approximately four miles to the west of Hailsham an ALG was laid near Deanland Wood with two grass runways. It opened in April 1944 with three Polish squadrons flying Spitfire IXs though it had already been in use as an emergency landing ground. [7]

The largest single offensive operation of this period was the famous, or infamous, Dieppe raid. Under pressure from the Russians to create a second front to help relieve the strain on the eastern front, the raid was a political, rather than military, necessity and as a consequence was a complete failure. The raid - code-named "Operation Jubilee" - was planned as a "reconnaissance in force" to test Hitler's Channel defences and as a rehearsal for the eventual re-invasion of Europe. Originally devised as a fifteen-hour, two-tide operation to occupy and hold the entire Dieppe area, it was scaled down to a one-tide, six-hour raid with the intention being, in Churchill's own words "to kill as many Germans as possible and to take prisoners." [8]

The men of the Canadian Second Corps, which was stationed across East Sussex, formed the main infantry strike force with Newhaven being the principle departure port. Some vessels also left from Shoreham. The Naval support came from Portsmouth. Included in the force were fifty of the new Churchill tanks from the 14th (Calgary) Tank Regiment as well as No.3 and No.4 Royal Marine Commando and a small number of United States Rangers.

The need for air superiority was fully understood and the raid was to be supported by the largest number of RAF aircraft yet employed in a single operation. Altogether sixty-eight squadrons were to fly 3,000 missions in the sixteen hours before and during the attack upon Dieppe.

In the early hours of 19 August 1942, 250 vessels crossed the Channel. The German defenders, however, were alerted before the landing craft even reached the beaches. Not a single tank was able to cross the beach. The large stones, of which the beach surface is composed, got inside the tracks and the tanks ground to a halt. Dieppe's defences were far too strong and only a handful of men managed to fight their way into town. The raid was a disaster. Of the 4,963 Canadians, only 2,120 returned to Newhaven, many of whom were severely wounded. All fifty tanks had to be abandoned along with thirty-three landing craft. (So much equipment was left behind that Hitler sarcastically thanked Britain for sending the Germans samples of all their weapons!). [9] The Navy suffered 550 casualties and one destroyer, H.M.S. *Berkeley*, was sunk. Major Pat Porteous of No.4 Commando and Major John Foote of the Royal Hamilton Light Infantry both won the Victoria Cross for their bravery at Dieppe.

The Spitfires of No. 131 Squadron from Merston flew four sorties on the day, three of which were over Dieppe, claiming a number of successes against Focke-Wolf 190s and Dornier 217s. From Friston the Hurricanes of Nos. 32 and 253 squadrons were used to attack the German gun emplacements supported by the Hurricanes of No.3 and 245 squadrons from Shoreham. In total the RAF lost 112 aircraft though forty-five airmen were rescued from the sea by the High Speed Launches which operated out of Newhaven. By comparison, the Luftwaffe lost only seventy-two aircraft and the ground troops suffered less than 600 casualties.

It is said that the Dieppe raid taught the Allies many valuable lessons. The first of these was that armoured vehicles capable of destroying pillboxes had to land with the assault troops. This led to the design of floating tanks which were highly successful during the D-Day landings. Secondly, it was realised that a frontal assault upon a fortified harbour was impracticable. The result of this was the development of the Mulberry artificial harbour which could be deployed off a beach away from strongly defended ports.

The districts between the ports of Newhaven and Portsmouth were designated a Concentration Area for the 1st and 30th Corps in preparation for Overlord. From February 1944 troops began to pour into Sussex. The 4th Armoured Brigade, consisting of the Royal Scots Greys, the 3rd County of London Yeomanry, the 44th Battalion The Royal Tank Regiment and the King's Royal Rifle Corps, arrived in the county on 10 February, establishing its headquarters at Worthing. Two months later the 27th Armoured Brigade moved into the Petworth - Ardingly area with Petworth House being taken over by the 13/18th Royal Hussars and the East Riding Yeomanry. Meanwhile, Wakehurst Place was occupied by the Staffordshire Yeomanry. A number of squadrons of this brigade were equipped with specially converted, and highly secret, amphibious Sherman Tanks which could make their own way ashore if launched from landing craft into deep water. The elite Guards Armoured Division was stationed in East Sussex. [10]

A soldier guarding the coast in 1940. (Imperial War Museum, H4607).

The cavalry was followed by the infantry in the form of the 15th Scottish Infantry Division which spread its brigades from Hove, through Lancing and Worthing to Ashington and Storrington. Divisional headquarters was at Knepp Castle near West Grinstead. There was also a Commando unit based at Littlehampton. Known as X Troop, it consisted predominantly of anti-Nazi escapees from Germany, including many Jews. Though its activities were highly classified, it is known that they included small-scale, cross-Channel raids and intelligence gathering. Amongst these missions were a series of raids on successive nights between the 15th and 18th of May to investigate the beach defences on the French coast. [11]

Across Sussex, particularly in the designated South Downs

A 12-pounder breech-loading gun in its emplacement on the cliff-top ramparts of Newhaven Fort, (TQ 448004). (By kind permission of Newhaven Fort).

Training Area and along the coast, the various regiments practised manoeuvres and beach landings throughout the spring of 1944. The south-facing slopes of the Downs between Clayton and Lewes were used by the Royal Navy for gunnery practice, firing inland from the sea. The Army also practised against the Downs, shooting from Ditchling Common into the nearby hills. Farmhouses in the area served as targets for the Canadian Army and most were damaged. They were re-built after the war at the Canadian's expense. [12]

The final large-scale rehearsal for Overlord, which took place on 4 May, was called *Exercise Fabius*. It involved the whole of the British 1st Corps, including the tanks of the armoured regiments as well as Royal Engineers and Marine Commandos, "attacking" the beach between Littlehampton and Bognor. Just a few weeks later, on 1 June, the troops were ordered to be ready for the start of the largest sea-borne assault ever undertaken. From that date onwards the invasion would take place as soon as sea and weather conditions were suitable.

During the build up for D-Day the coast from Pagham Harbour round to the eastern edge of Selsey was subject to the tightest security. Unauthorised civilians were banned from the area and fishing vessels were excluded from the seas around Pagham Harbour. Within this area the component parts of one of the famous Mulberry harbours was assembled. (The other Mulberry assembly area was off Dungeness). These unique structures were complete floating harbours comprising quays, jetties and breakwaters. The harbours were to be towed out to lie off the Normandy coast immediately after D-Day which, on 26 May, was scheduled for 5 June. These were massive structures and more than 400 component parts had to be towed across the Channel with a total weight of 1,500,000 tons. [13]

With the date having been decided, all the troops were confined to camp, the Concentration Areas and Marshalling Areas were sealed with barbed wire - many also posted armed guards. During the last days of May the roads of Sussex were filled with convoys of troops and armoured vehicles. The troops in transit were not permitted to speak with civilians. By 1 June the towns and villages where the troops had spent the previous weeks were empty and quiet as the various regiments were now at their Marshalling Areas near to Newhaven, Shoreham and Portsmouth. The units that were to embark at Newhaven and Shoreham were placed into Marshalling Area J. This stretched from Seaford to Brighton and extended as far inland as Haywards Heath. Within this area were ten major Marshalling Camps, at such places as Firle Park, Stanmer Park and Borde Hill, with a total capacity of 15,000 men and more than 2,000 vehicles. Sussex became a vast car park.

Village greens were used to park military vehicles and dual carriageways were closed off on one side and used as hard standing for tanks. Each Allied vehicle was painted with a large white star on the sides and roof to aid identification.

By 4 June, the troops had moved down to the ports and some had already embarked upon their landing craft, many of which had been made in Sussex at Littlehampton, Itchenor and Bosham. But the fine, still weather had changed to strong winds and heavy cloud with the possibility of rain storms. It was decided at Supreme Headquarters to postpone the invasion for one day in the hope that the weather would improve. Fortunately the weather did settle into another period of good weather and 6 June was declared D-Day.

Throughout the night of 5/6 June the Sussex skies were filled with the dark silhouettes of thousands of allied aircraft. Along the Sussex coast a series of "Eureka" navigational beacons and lights guided the bombers and transports from their bases in Oxfordshire, Berkshire, Wiltshire and Devon to the aerial rendezvous points above Worthing, Littlehampton and Bognor, before setting out across the Channel. The 6th Airborne Division passed over Worthing but two of its Horsa Gliders, packed with troops, failed to reach France. One landed in Worthing and the other nearby at Sompting.

From Newhaven and Shoreham the ships sailed with their human and armoured cargoes. Through Littlehampton went vessels loaded with ammunition, and from Pagham the Mulberry harbours were towed slowly across the Channel.

It was now time for the Sussex airfields to play their part in Operation Overlord. The objective was to form a screen of Allied fighters around the entire invasion area beginning at 04.25 on the morning of 6 June. High cover was to be provided by the USAF and low cover by the RAF. The Allied fighters also supplied escorts for almost every other air activity, from bombing missions to coastal patrols and airborne assault.

From Tangmere the Spitfires of six squadrons of the Royal Canadian Air Force provided air cover for the troops on the landing beaches and they patrolled further inland to prevent German aerial counter-attacks. For D-Day, Ford was also the base for six squadrons of Spitfire IX LFs. These protected the landing craft as well as the beaches and the surrounding skies. A single squadron of Typhoons at Westhampnett patrolled the skies over the beaches whilst the six squadrons of Typhoons from Thorney Island (including No. 164 Squadron which was composed partly of Argentinean pilots and No. 193 Squadron with mostly Brazilian flyers) was given the task of ground attack to prevent enemy reinforcements reaching the invasion coast.

The Free French airforce, flying Spitfire IXBs, based three squadrons at Merston and on D-Day these provided low-level cover for the troop transport vessels. Another Free French squadron was at Shoreham and on 6 June its Spitfire VBs escorted the gliders of the Airborne troops. At Friston was a Belgian squadron (No. 350) which, with No. 501 squadron, flew sorties over the landing beaches throughout the day of 6 June.

The Advanced Landing Grounds, which had been upgraded for D-Day, were brought into the action. A second Belgian squadron of Spitfires, with a New Zealand and a South African squadron, was stationed at Selsey. Selsey's three squadrons, three Czechoslovakian squadrons from Apuldram and Chailey's Polish squadrons provided low-level cover over the beaches.

Of the three Spitfire squadrons that operated out of Deanland, No.611 patrolled the Normandy beaches, whilst No.

64 Squadron and No. 234 Squadron escorted airborne divisions to their drop zones. Coolham's and Funtingdon's six squadrons of Mustangs formed part of the "Pool of Readiness" which could be drawn upon if the air cover over the landing area was breached. All six squadrons were called into action.

Funtingdon's Mustangs escorted Beaufighters of Coastal Command on anti-submarine patrols and Coolham's three squadrons were used to escort a formation of tugs and gliders. From Hammerwood, No. 659 Squadron Air Observation Post flew Auster Mark IV spotter planes, but their precise duties are not known.[14] To help avoid mistakes in the crowded skies over Normandy, black and white stripes were painted on the wings and fuselages of the Allied aircraft.

The following is the order of battle for the Sussex-based squadrons in June 1944:-[15]

AIRFIELD	SQUADRONS	AIRCRAFT	WING
Thorney Island	198	Typhoon	123
	609	Typhoon	123
	164	Typhoon	136
	183	Typhoon	136
Westhampnett	184	Typhoon	129
Ford	441	Spitfire IX LF	144
	442	Spitfire IX LF	144
	443	Spitfire IX LF	144
	132	Spitfire IX LF	125
	602	Spitfire IX LF	125
	453	Spitfire IX LF	125
	456	Mosquito	85 Group Night Fighter Force.

Funtingdon	19	Mustang III	122		Shoreham	345	Spitfire V LF	
	65	Mustang III	122			277	Walrus	Air Sea Rescue
	122	Mustang III	122					
Tangmere	401	Spitfire IX LF	126		Friston	350	Spitfire V LF	
	411	Spitfire IX LF	126			501	Spitfire V LF	
	412	Spitfire IX LF	126					
	103	Spitfire IX LF	127		Deanland	64	Spitfire V LF	
	416	Spitfire IX LF	127			234	Spitfire V LF	
	421	Spitfire IX LF	127			611	Spitfire V LF	
Selsey	302	Spitfire IX LF	131					
	308	Spitfire IX LF	131					
	317	Spitfire IX LF	131					
Coolham	129	Mustang III	133					
	306	Mustang III	133					
	315	Mustang III	133					
Chailey	222	Spitfire IX LF	135					
	349	Spitfire IX LF	135					
	485	Spitfire IX LF	135					
Bognor	66	Spitfire IX LF	132					
	331	Spitfire IX LF	132					
	332	Spitfire IX LF	132					
Apuldram	310	Spitfire IX LF	134					
	312	Spitfire IX LF	134					
	313	Spitfire IX LF	134					
Merston	329	Spitfire IX LF	145					
	340	Spitfire IX LF	145					
	341	Spitfire IX LF	145					
Gatwick	2	Mustang II	35					
	4	Spitfire PRX1	35					
	268	Mustang 1A	35					

The value of the previous two years of attacks against the German air capacity was clearly demonstrated by the fact that on D-Day the enemy were able to mount less than a hundred sorties. As a consequence D-Day was a success but it was another year before the Germans surrendered. In the days following D-Day the beach-heads were expanded and the Allies drove deeper into France.

The Sussex airfields continued to play a major role in keeping the Luftwaffe at bay and in attacking enemy ground troops and supply lines. But gradually, as the war moved away from the coast, airfields were established in France and many of the Sussex-based squadrons transferred across the Channel. Newhaven continued to be a departure point for troops and provisions for many months after D-Day, whilst Littlehampton became an important ammunition supply port.

Sussex now prepared itself to receive casualties from the battle for Normandy. Emergency Medical Service wards were erected at the Royal West Sussex Hospital and the St. Richards Hospital in Chichester (the latter being reserved for wounded German prisoners-of-war). Two wards were also made available for D-Day casualties at the Graylingwell Mental Hospital. Emergency transport for the wounded was provided by Southdown buses whose vehicles were converted to ambulances by the removal of the seats and the addition of stretcher slings. The hospitals were soon filled to over-capacity and this situation continued until Field Hospitals were set up in France.

A new terror now appeared in the skies over Sussex - the V1. Around a 1,000 of these flying-bombs fell around the county, causing much damage. Fast fighters, such as the Spitfire and the Typhoon, were able to intercept the V1 and many were shot down. However, the V1 was superseded by the V2 rocket against which there was no defence. Fortunately for the people of Sussex only four of these missiles hit the county.

Throughout the course of the war, more than 103,000 bombs of all descriptions had dropped on Sussex and 4,910 people were killed or injured. [16] After the war most of the A.L.G.s were returned to agricultural use. Of the principal airfields Westhampnett is now known as Goodwood airfield and is used by civilian light aircraft whilst Shoreham continues to thrive as a small commercial airport.

A WWII hangar at the former Ford airfield which is now in the grounds of H.M.P. Ford, (SU 998027). (By kind permission of the Governor, H.M.P. Ford).

Tangmere continued to be an important part of the re-formed Fighter Command with two squadrons of Gloster Meteor jet fighters in residence through the 1940s. In the 1950s the Meteors were superseded by Hawker Hunters of Nos.1 and 34 squadrons. In 1958 Tangmere was taken over by Signals Command, with their Cannberra and Varsity aircraft.

The airfield was closed in 1970. In 1945 Ford airfield was returned to the Royal Navy, once again adopting the name of H.M.S. *Peregrine*. It remained a training and experimental establishment until 1958. Thorney Island continued after the war as an Air-Sea Warfare Development base before becoming the home of the 47th Regiment of the Royal Artillery.

11
The Sussex Soldier

The men of Sussex had been defending their communities long before the dawn of history, but it was not until the formation of the militia that the men were organised and trained to act as soldiers in the modern sense of the word. Until the New Model Army set the foundations for a national army, these "trained bands" were England's principle military force.

A remnant of the feudal system of obligatory military duty, every male between the ages of sixteen and sixty was, theoretically, required to serve in the militia. Though dating back as far as the Anglo-Saxon fyrd, service in the militia was not established in law until Edward I's Statute of Windsor in 1285. This item of legislation formulated the Commissions of Array which became the standard method of raising a field army from the shire levies.

This act was repealed in 1558 and each individual's military obligations were re-defined based on their financial status. Thus a man worth only £5 to £10 a year was expected to provide just a coat of plated armour, a pike or halberd, a longbow and a helmet, whereas those worth £1,000 or more were obliged to supply sixteen horses, eighty suits of light armour, forty pikes, thirty bows, twenty bills or halberds, twenty arquebuses and fifty helmets.[1]

Responsibility for the organisation of the militia and the defence of Sussex rested with the Lord Lieutenants of the county. Much of this responsibility was delegated to deputy-lieutenants, who were originally chosen by the Privy Council but, after 1625, were selected by the Lord Lieutenants. It was the duty of the Justices of the Peace to ensure that the constables in their respective rapes mustered the militia, with the assistance of the county muster-master who was an experienced, professional soldier.

Each Sussex rape mustered four companies of foot of 100 men each, plus Chichester had a company of its own. In addition to these twenty-five companies of foot, all of the six rapes also had a company of cavalry, each with a theoretical strength of fifty mounted men. Of the four foot companies of each rape, two were regarded as front line troops made up of the best men with the best weapons and were known as the "selected" companies. The two non-selected companies were seen as second-rate formations and were poorly armed and usually under-strength.

Companies were commanded by captains, some of whom were JPs, but most of whom were drawn from the local landed gentry. A knight was normally in charge of the cavalry. Captains were chosen by the Lord Lieutenants. In 1626 a pioneer company was raised from each rape from men of gentry status led by a specifically appointed captain of pioneers. There was no financial reward for holding militia appointments (other than for the muster-master which was a paid position) but it allowed ambitious men to make the acquaintance of the most influential people in the county.

The annual muster, the frequency of which could be increased if there was a perceived danger, was usually staged at the same place in each rape, such as Ditchling Common for the Lewes rape and Berwick Common for the Pevensey rape. The horse companies, of which there was just one per rape, mustered together at Bury Hill in West Sussex and Piltdown in the east. Training also took place in local, smaller groups (of no more than twenty) in the weeks preceding the annual muster.

In 1625 the process of selection was abolished and each captain was given a district, or hundred, from which he had to raise his company and this led to an increase in the county's military strength. In 1638, the Sussex trained bands of foot totalled 2,804 men. By this time more men were armed with muskets than with pikes or corslets, whereas twenty years earlier many men were only expected to provide a pike or a half share in a musket.

The cavalry (later to be known as the yeomanry) was composed of men of substance. Those persons with an annual income of at least two hundred pounds were expected to be mounted and armed. However, the deputy-lieutenants were reluctant to force military service upon men who were not only their social equals, but also their friends and neighbours. As a result there were many defaulters at the muster and the county could not raise even 200 cavalrymen. Part of the problem was that there was no actual law which enforced military service as James I had abolished the earlier reforms and reinstated the Statute of Windsor. This was not resolved until the passing of the 1662 Militia Act.

The militia was put on a more standardised basis in 1757 when Parliament ordered each county to recruit a specific number of troops with the men being selected for duty through a compulsory ballot. These men were trained for one month a year and, for the first time, they were paid for their military service through local taxation.

In the absence of a police force one of the principle functions of the militia and the yeomanry was to keep the public peace. This included helping with the control of smuggling, which was endemic along the Sussex coast.

During the Napoleonic Wars the nature of the militia changed. A Supplementary Militia Act in 1796 required a large increase in the militia. Troops were raised in proportion to the population of each area with the larger towns and cities mustering entire battalions. These "regular" militiamen were enlisted for five years. They were continuously under arms and were garrisoned away from their homes, though they were not required to serve overseas. Substitutes were permitted and many who could afford to do so paid others to perform their military service. Service in the militia continued to be a compulsory duty until the middle of the nineteenth century when the Militia Act of 1852 made recruitment voluntary. [2]

Wealthy gentlemen were also encouraged to form their own "volunteer" militia corps. Probably the most famous of these units was the Cinque Ports Volunteers which was formed and led by William Pitt during his period as Warden of the Cinque Ports. Those that joined the volunteers were exempt for service in the militia. Sussex and a part of Kent formed the Southern Military District. The total number of volunteer troops in this district, including the Cinque Ports volunteers, was counted in January 1804 at 1,521 Cavalry and 10,257 Infantry. [3]

The Napoleonic Wars also saw a huge number of regular soldiers march into Sussex. During this time Horsham became an important staging post as it was situated at the cross-roads of two military routes i.e. between London and the south coast, and between the naval ports of Chatham and Portsmouth. Large barracks were built in 1797 on the road from Horsham to Worthing but often these could not accommodate all the troops that stopped at Horsham and many regiments had to camp on the common, which was on the northern side of the town. During the nineteen years of its existence the Horsham Barracks saw no less than sixty-nine different regiments pass through its gates. It was at Horsham that one of the most famous regiments of the British Army was first raised. In 1800, a body of volunteers from fourteen other regiments met at Horsham (later moving to Blatchington Barracks) to make up the Experimental Corps of Riflemen. This unit, the first regular body of rifle-armed troops in the British Army, went on to become the 95th Rifles and then the Rifle Brigade. It continues in existence today as the Royal Greenjackets. [4]

Other barracks were built in towns around Sussex, notably at Arundel, Bognor Regis, Chichester, Petworth, Shoreham, Littlehampton, Pevensey, Hastings, Winchelsea, Lewes, Hailsham, Blatchington, Eastbourne, and East Grinstead. The barracks at Bexhill-on-Sea became the home of the King's German Legion, (K.G.L.). This body was composed predominantly from soldiers of the Hanoverian Army who had escaped to England when Napoleon over-ran the Electorate in 1803. At that time the King of England was still the Elector of Hanover. Bexhill remained the base for the K.G.L. for ten years during which time close links were established with the community. (including 108 local girls who married German soldiers), which continue to this day.

In 1794 the Somerset and Oxford militias were sent to Blatchington Barracks near Seaford. The local shopkeepers took advantage of this influx of new customers by raising prices and selling old produce no longer fit for human consumption. Soon men began to fall ill and, inevitably, the starving troops took matters into their own hands. 500 men of the Oxford Militia marched into the town and seized all the bread, flour and meat they could find. Intoxicated with their easy victory over the shopkeepers the mutineers then marched to Tide Mills, stealing more grain and forcing a ship carrying flour to unload its cargo at Newhaven. The following day regular troops marched into Newhaven and, accompanied by the local Seaford Volunteers, restored order. The supposed ringleaders were tried at Horsham assizes and four were later executed. [5]

The largest concentration of troops in Sussex during the Napoleonic Wars was at Brighton. At the 1793 training camp at Brighton were regiments of Volunteer Militia from twelve counties, including Sussex, plus a regiment of artillery and the 10th (Prince of Wales Own) Regiment of Light Dragoons, making a total of some 10,000 troops .[6]

Later in the nineteenth century even larger encampments were formed at Brighton. In 1861, around 15,000 Volunteer Militia took part in a mock attack upon Ovingdean and the following year almost 20,000 troops entertained large crowds in exercises on Race Hill. Amongst these troops were members of the Sussex Volunteer Rifles and the Sussex Volunteer Artillery.

Regular troops were also posted to Brighton, being accommodated in the Infantry Barracks in Church Street and the Cavalry Barracks on the Lewes Road in Preston. Possibly the most famous regiment to have been quartered in the Cavalry

Barracks was the 11th (Prince Albert's) Regiment of Hussars. Led to the Crimean War by their Colonel, the Earl of Cardigan (who lived at 45 Brunswick Square), the 11th Hussars charged into the Valley of Death with the other regiments of the Light Brigade at Balaclava in 1854. [7]

The militia, the volunteers and the Army remained separate entities until the reforms of the Secretary of State for War, Edward Cardwell, in the 1870's. The reforms brought the local militia and volunteers together under the administration of the regular Army regiments. To help maintain a strong local identity the regular regiments were provided with a permanent barracks within the county to which they were affiliated. In Sussex this led to the building of the Roussillion Barracks in Chichester. This became the Regimental Depot of the Royal Sussex Regiment and the headquarters of the Sussex militia and volunteer battalions. Recruitment had always been a problem for the British Army and with these measures Cardwell hoped that the closer ties between the part-time and the full-time troops would encourage more volunteers and militiamen to turn professional.

The last major re-structuring of Britain's part-time forces came in April 1908. The militia and the volunteers were abolished and incorporated into a new voluntary body, the Territorial Army. The distinctions between the regulars and the part-timers were swept away with the Territorials being, quite simply, the reserve forces of the British Army, their title later becoming the Territorial Army Volunteer Reserve.

The principle of independent volunteer units was revised in May 1940 when the expectation of a sudden invasion by German forces led to a call for men to form units of "Local Defence Volunteers". The original intention was to encourage men with previous military experience to join the LDV, initially to counter paratroop landings and one of their early nicknames was the "Parashooters". [8] Though the age range for acceptance into the LDV was seventeen to sixty-five, it was not uncommon for men in their seventies and boys of fifteen to sign up. Around a third of all recruits were ex-soldiers. At first only British subjects were eligible for the LDV. It was expected that nationally 500,000 men might volunteer yet by the end of June almost one and a half million men had joined up.

Command of the West Sussex forces was handed to a former Grenadier Guard, and the Group Commander of East Sussex was Captain Madden of the Somerset Light Infantry. LDV headquarters for the eastern half of the county was at Lewes and at Chichester for West Sussex. Most company and platoon commanders were ex-officers though some were simply men of standing in the local community.

The Sussex LDV, or Home Guard as they were known from 31 July, eventually numbered twenty-six battalions with each battalion being composed of at least four companies of, usually, four platoons. The Battalion districts were:-

No.1 Chichester   No.2 Petworth   3. Horsham   4. Billingshurst 5. Worthing 6. Arundel/Amberley 7. Midhurst 8. Bognor Regis and Selsey   9. Shoreham-By-Sea   10. East Brighton 13. Haywards Heath 14. Hove 15. West Brighton 16. Lewes 17. East Grinstead 18 Crowborough 19. Burwash 20. Hailsham 21. Eastbourne 22. Rye 23. Hastings/Bexhill 24. Uckfield 26. Worth Forest.

These were general service battalions, in addition to which there were three specialist Battalions: the 11th (39th GPO) Battalion which was a signals unit, the 12th (2nd Southdown Motor Transport) Battalion, and the 25th (2nd Southern Railway). The last two were, of course, responsible for defending the means of transportation across Sussex and the neighbouring counties. By 23 June 1940, nearly 17,000 employees of the Southern Railway had volunteered for the LDV throughout Sussex, Kent and Surrey. Sadly they had only 400 rifles between them! Amongst the more unusual Home Guard units was the Lewes Home Guard Cavalry. Composed of former jockeys, huntsmen and landowners, this elite force at one time included more than fifty mounted members. There was also a Sussex Recovery Company formed by Caffyns Garages, with five platoons based around the county. The duties of these platoons

included the provision of mechanics and recovery vehicles for the armed forces in the area. The Recovery Company was also responsible for keeping the roads open. [9]

A number of highly secret "Auxiliary" units were created across Sussex. Carefully selected from men with great knowledge of their locality, such as gamekeepers, this was a highly trained corps. In the event of a successful German landing, the Auxilliaries were to disappear into secret hides which had been stocked with food, weapons and ammunition. These men would then slip out of their hides at night to harass the invaders. Their life expectancy was just two weeks after they began their clandestine operations. [10]

A tunic of a sergeant of the Royal Sussex Regiment from 1876. On the tunic is the Indian Mutiny campaign medal of 1857-8. The tunic is on display in the Combined Services Museum, Eastbourne Redoubt. (By kind permission of the Sussex Combined Services Museum, Eastbourne Redoubt).

Apart from the age restrictions, all that was required of volunteers was that they should be reasonably fit, and men from all walks of life joined up. Schools and church halls were usually taken over as Platoon or Company headquarters though at Hove, rooms in the County Cricket Ground were used and at Storrington an evacuated monastery was re-occupied by the local Home Guard.

In the early days the poorly-armed Home Guard was not considered to be a fighting force and its duties were limited to observing and reporting enemy incursions, acting as local guides for the regular troops and guarding essential services and installations such as post offices, telephone exchanges, train stations and public utilities. The men were expected to patrol every night for between two to four hours. So from the tops of church towers, water towers, castles and hill tops, the Home Guard maintained a twenty-four hour watch over the towns and villages of Sussex.

As so much equipment had been abandoned at Dunkirk there was a serious shortage of weapons in Britain in 1940. Those rifles that were available were reserved for the regular troops. At first the men of the LDV supplied their own arms but gradually rifles were issued to each platoon, the men sharing the weapons as they took their turns on the nightly patrols. Initially the volunteers received an "LDV" arm band with possibly a forage cap and those khaki uniforms were that sent to the Home Guard had to be, like the rifles, shared by the men.

The voluntary nature of the force changed in December 1941 when all men between the ages of eighteen and fifty-one became liable for service in the Home Guard. The structure of the Home Guard was also put on a more formal setting with commissions being granted to the senior company and platoon commanders. Gradually the Home Guard developed into a sophisticated defensive force. As well as rifles, uniforms and steel helmets, limited numbers of general purpose machine guns, Bren Guns, Spigot mortars, grenades and even 2lb Anti-Tank guns were issued to the battalions. The Home Guard was also now expected to use this weaponry against the enemy and their role now included that of local defence. This included Anti-Aircraft duties which at last gave the men a chance to fire their guns in anger. The Home Guard also took over the Coastal Defence batteries, releasing the Royal Artillery gun crews for overseas service. On 31 December 1944, the Home Guard was stood down.

Regular troops also formed part of the defensive forces during World War II. In May 1940, the 45th Infantry Division was

A photograph of the 1905 camp of the Sussex Yeomanry at Lewes.

moved from the West Country to guard the Sussex coast from Rye to Bognor. After the evacuation of the British and allied armies from Dunkirk the defence of Sussex, Kent and areas of Surrey was undertaken by the recently formed 12 Corps whose headquarters was at Tunbridge Wells. The 45th Division was incorporated into the 12th Division and was then concentrated between Rye and Newhaven, with the 1st Motorised Machine Gun Brigade posted between Brighton and Shoreham. In reserve was the 7th Corps which was placed between East Grinstead and Reigate. In February 1941, responsibility for the defence of the Sussex coast was entrusted to the First Canadian Corps with 12 Corps now being responsible only for Kent.

The Canadian First Division was stationed in West Sussex, with the Canadian Second Division, comprising the 4th, 5th and 6th Infantry Brigades holding the eastern part of the country. The most easterly of these formations was the 4th Brigade, with the Royal Regiment of Canada occupying the beach defences between Rye and Winchelsea, the Royal Hamilton Light Infantry posted at Hastings, and the Essex Scottish Regiment, along with the 14th Canadian Army Tank Regiment (Calgary), held in reserve at Battle. The 6th Brigade was posted further west, with the Queen's Own Cameron Highlanders of Canada and Les Fusiliers Mont-Royal at Newhaven. The 6th Brigade's reserve was the South Saskatchewan Regiment which was at Lewes.

After World War II the coastal defences were abandoned by the army. Newhaven Fort, however, continued under military authority with "B" Troop, 223 Independent Maintenance Battery forming the garrison of just seven men. The fort was taken over by the Battlefield Clearance Unit in 1957 and finally handed to the civilian authorities in 1962.

The principle regular army regiment to bear the name of Sussex was the 35th Regiment of Foot. Raised in Belfast in 1701 by the Earl of Donegal (whose name, coincidentally, was Arthur Chichester!) the 35th was granted the unique honour by William III (of Orange) of being allowed to wear orange facings on its uniform. This link with the Dutch Royal house was re-established later in the regiment's history when Queen Juliana of

the Netherlands was appointed Colonel-in-Chief in 1953. It was not until 1787, however, that the regiment became associated with Sussex.

This happened because the colonel of the regiment was then the Duke of Richmond and he began recruiting men from his estates in Sussex. At this time the 35th was the Dorsetshire Regiment and it was the 25th Regiment that carried the title "Sussex". The Duke was permitted to take the Sussex name for the 35th and from 1804 the 35th became the Sussex Regiment and in 1832 the Royal Sussex Regiment, its facing colours then changing to royal blue. In those days the regiments were rarely stationed in their affiliated counties when serving in the UK. The troops were moved around Britain to keep the peace, never staying long in one place in case they formed attachments with the locals which might prejudice their policing duties.

Like so many county regiments, the Royal Sussex had a long and distinguished service record. Its campaigns include actions in the capture of Quebec, the American War of Independence, the Napoleonic Wars, the Indian Mutiny, the Boer War, the relief of Khartoum and the two World Wars.

During the period of the Indian Mutiny the regiment became associated with the 107th (Bengal Infantry) which was one of the regiments of the East India Company. The East India Company's army was transferred to the British service in 1861 and twelve years later the 107th was brigaded with the 35th at Chichester Barracks which became the Brigade Depot. In 1881, the 35th and 107th were amalgamated to become the 1st and 2nd Battalions, Royal Sussex Regiment.

In World War I, the regiment was increased to twenty-three battalions, which included the local Territorial battalions. Of these, the 3rd (Militia) Battalion remained at Newhaven throughout the war from where reinforcements were sent to join the other battalions overseas. In WWII, the 2nd, 4th and 5th Battalions formed the Royal Sussex Brigade which formed part of the British Expeditionary Force that went to France in 1940 and which was rescued from the beaches at Dunkirk.

The 2nd Battalion was later converted into the 10th Parachute Battalion. The 1st Battalion was in Egypt at the outbreak of the war and it fought in the Middle East and the Mediterranean theatres until the end of hostilities. After the war the regiment saw action in the Middle East and Korea. [11]

The regiment's independent existence came to an end in 1966 when it was amalgamated with the Surrey, Middlesex and two Kent regiments (the Buffs and the Royal Kent) to form the Queen's Regiment. This regiment is now the Princess of Wales's Royal Regiment. [12]

The local volunteers first served abroad when they joined the Sussex Regiment in the Boer War. In 1908 the volunteers formed the new Territorial Army and in Sussex they constituted the 4th Battalion and 5th (Cinque Ports) Battalion of the Royal Sussex Regiment. The 4th Battalion was based in West Sussex and the 5th in East Sussex. In WWI both these battalions fought on the Western Front, the 4th also serving at Gallipoli and in Palestine.

After WWII, the 4th and 5th Battalions joined forces to become the 4/5th (Cinque Ports) Battalion, Territorial Army. This unit was disbanded in 1967 after the Queen's Regiment had been formed. The proud tradition of the Sussex Volunteers lives on, however, in the TA companies of the 3rd Battalion of The Princess of Wales's Royal Regiment which still carry the Sussex name.

A unit of Engineers, the 1st Sussex Royal Engineer Volunteers, was also formed in Sussex. Raised at Eastbourne in 1890, its headquarters was originally at the Eastbourne Redoubt. Over the course of the following few years volunteer companies were formed throughout the county and by the time of the Boer War twelve companies had been established.

The Volunteer Engineers were disbanded on 31 March 1908 and the next day were incorporated into the Territorial Army. As part of the 1st Home Counties Division, and later the 8th and 5th Divisions, the Sussex Engineers served in India and the Western Front from 1914 until the end of WWI. In WWII the Sussex Engineers, then listed as the 44th (Home Counties) Divisional Royal Engineers, with its headquarters at Queen Square in Brighton, fought in France in 1940, being rescued from the Dunkirk beaches with the rest of the BEF. The Engineers were then sent to North Africa where they took part in the Battle of El Alamein and the invasion of Scilly. The unit returned to England in 1943 and joined the 30th Corps for D-Day.

In 1947 the Territorial Army was reformed and the Sussex Engineers formed part of the 119th Field Engineer Regiment. Its headquarters remained at Queen Square, the unit also occupying the former cavalry barracks at Preston. The long existence of the Sussex Engineers ended in March 1967.

The artillery is currently represented in Sussex by the 47th (Hampshire and Sussex) Regiment of Artillery which is based at Baker Barracks on Thorney Island. Prior to 1939 there had been two artillery regiments based in and around Sussex. The first was the 58th (Sussex) Field Regiment R.A. (T.A.), with batteries at Hastings and Eastbourne and the 98th (Surrey and Sussex Yeomanry) Field Regiment, with batteries at Brighton and Chichester. In June 1939, the 114th Field Regiment R.A. (T.A.) was raised with a cadre of experienced officers and N.C.O.s from the 58th. The 114th was disbanded at the end of the war.

Another Territorial Army unit, the 200 (The Sussex Yeomanry) Field Battery, was formed in 1967 at Brighton. [13] This unit is all that remains of what was The Sussex Yeomanry Regiment which was originally Sussex's volunteer cavalry force. Raised in the closing months of the Boer War as the 1st Sussex Yeomanry, the regiment never saw action as a mounted corps. When the Territorial Army was formed in 1908, the regiment was brigaded with the Royal East Kent Mounted Rifles and the West Kent Yeomanry to form the South-Eastern Mounted Brigade.

This brigade was mobilised in August 1914 at the outbreak of WWI but, because of a shortage of horses and a desperate need for infantry, the men were invited to participate in the Gallipoli campaign as dismounted cavalry. From Turkey the regiment went

Bexhill Barracks. Above the door is the badge of the Royal Sussex Regiment. The barracks are on the A259 in the Old Town area of Bexhill, (TQ 737080).

The Keep of the Roussillion Barracks on the A286 to the north of Chichester, (SU 895065).

to Egypt and Palestine. At this time the regiment was converted into an infantry battalion, as were other yeomanry regiments. Thus, on 3 January 1917, the 16th (Sussex Yeomanry) Battalion, Royal Sussex Regiment, was created. The battalion was transferred to France in May 1918 where it fought until the end of the war.

In WWII the Sussex Yeomanry, having been a cavalry corps and then an infantry regiment, became an artillery battery which, with the Surrey Yeomanry, became the 98th Field Regiment. Remarkably, in 1993, this unit then joined the engineers - becoming the 127 (Sussex Yeomanry) Squadron Royal Engineers T.A.

12
Sussex's Military Heritage

Sussex has many sites of military interest, though most of these sites are in the southern half of the county - particularly along the coast and across the South Downs. Almost all of these places are readily accessible to the general public.

The Causewayed Enclosures of Neolithic man are now barely discernible though the camp at Coombe Hill, near Willingdon (map reference TQ 575023) can still be accurately traced. Far more rewarding are the Celtic structures of the Iron Age. The towering ramparts of Cissbury Ring (TQ 140080) are impressive reminders of the importance that our Celtic forebears placed upon defence. Like all the Downland forts, Cissbury is situated on the top of a steep-sided hill with magnificent views along the Downs. All the hill forts offer great walks and breath-taking scenery. Chanctonbury Ring (TQ 139121), Wolstonbury Hill (TQ 284138), Devil's Dyke (TQ 260121), Hollingbury Castle (TQ 322078), Highdown (TQ 093040), Mount Caburn (TQ 445089), Harting Down (SU 807185), and The Trundle (SU 877110) are all worthy of a visit. Each one displays the same characteristics of a ditch and rampart though some, such as Hollingbury and Harting Down, have suffered severely from the ravages of time. Mount Caburn was also used as a lookout post by the Home Guard in World War II and the army built huts on the summit of Highdown Hill in 1940. Many of these sites are preserved by the National Trust and all are free to the general public.

At the coastal hill forts at Seaford Head (TV 495978) and Belle Tout (TV 560958), little is to be seen of the defensive works. Originally a mile or two from the coast, these forts, and the chalk cliffs upon which they sit, are crumbling into the sea. The views along the cliffs, however, are amongst the finest in England.

The most accessible, and certainly the most remarkable, of the Wealden promontory forts is High Rocks. Situated on the border with Kent, near Tunbridge Wells (TQ 561381), the fort was formed on top of a sandstone outcrop which has eroded into a maze of gullies and fissures. The earthen ramparts which secured the rear of the fort were excavated but have now been re-covered and are no longer obvious to the eye. There is a small entry fee to High Rocks.

Another series of Celtic remains which may have had a military purpose are the Chichester Dykes. Although they run intermittently all the way from near Halnaker (SU 880095) to beyond Mid Lavant (SU 835081) the Dykes are now reduced to a shallow cutting.

The Romans have left us the great castle at Pevensey. Encompassing more than 1,700 years of military history, this is one of the premier sites in Sussex. Much of the old Roman walls, with their D-shaped bastions, still remain and it was within these defences that William of Normandy established his first base camp before passing on to Hastings.

William later built a typically Norman motte and bailey castle here. The visitor today, however, sees an imposing inner bailey of a medieval castle which was besieged four times but never taken by assault. Amongst its attractions are collections of large catapult stones that were found around the site and may have been used in the sieges of the castle in the middle ages. In the grounds of the inner bailey is one of two demi-culverns that were placed in a battery on the south side of the outer bailey where the sea once lapped up to the foot of the walls. These cannon were listed as the armament of the castle in 1587, the year before the Spanish Armada. The castle was re-occupied in World War II by units of the British, Canadian and United States military as well as the local Home Guard. The towers of the castle were converted into barracks and an anti-tank gun embrasure and pillboxes for machine guns, which can still be seen, were integrated into the ruins of the keep.

The other principle military site of Roman times was the fortified city of Chichester. It is possible to walk round the old city walls (restored in the middle ages) along the top of an earthen rampart which was formed against the insides of the walls in the 18th century. The D-shaped bastions, which were added to the walls at some time during the fourth century, were designed to carry ballistae. Only five of the original bastions are now above ground. All that remains of Chichester castle is the motte which stands inside the north-eastern quarter of the city. The heights known as The Broyle, where the Parliamentarians established their camp during the siege of 1642, can be seen beyond the walls to the north of the city.

The Saxons have left little to remind us of their military prowess. However, the remains of one of Alfred the Great's "burgs" can be seen at Burpham to the north-east of Arundel (TQ 039085). The burg, now a cricket pitch, commands a bend in the River Arun and its ditch and steep rampart still represent a formidable obstacle.

Saxon England was swept away in the Norman conquest, though the visible remains of their oppressive feudalism can be seen across the county. As well as Pevensey, the castles at Hastings, Lewes, Bramber and Arundel all date from the eleventh century.

There is still something to be seen at Hastings. The castle sits high above the town (TV 822094) and has suffered considerably from the ravages of coastal erosion. Hastings was a promontory castle, built upon the top of a steep cliff made inaccessible from the landward side by a large ditch cut through the rock. The great tower has disappeared but parts of the main bailey wall still stand as well as the remains of the east gatehouse towers.

Bramber castle (TQ 184107) is free to the public as most of the stonework was taken to construct roads in the area. The central motte can still be seen with a few scant pieces of the bailey wall. One side of the gate-tower stands high above the bailey indicating just how imposing this structure once was.

Much more remains of Lewes castle (TQ 414101). With the aid of an audio tour the visitor can examine the remains of the shell keep and part of the bailey. It's most notable feature is the 14th century barbican which is still a public thoroughfare. Behind the barbican is the original Norman gatehouse. The larger part of the bailey, which was formerly a tilting-ground for the medieval knights, is now a bowling green and the castle's second motte, the Brack Mount, stands empty and isolated to the north-east. Short sections of the old town walls can still be seen, particularly to the north and west of the castle.

Arundel Castle, ruined in the Civil War, was restored to its present magnificent state in the 19th century. The most important remains from its medieval past are a Norman keep and gatehouse and a 13th century barbican. These can be viewed from the castle grounds (TQ 017074). Inside the castle is an armoury. Sadly few of the exhibits in the armoury have any connection with Arundel's history, though pikes, bills, swords, muskets, crossbows, suits of armour and Civil War helmets can be seen at close quarters. In one of the other rooms - the South Passage - pole arms and breast plates are also on display. Like Pevensey castle, the military occupied Arundel castle in WW II. An Observer Corps post was set up on the keep and the East Wing of the castle was used for officer accommodation - the troops were under canvas in the grounds.

At Church Norton on the south-western edge of Pagham Harbour (SZ 870959) is a Norman ringwork. It consists of a large mound with a ditch that embraces its front and sides. It may have been topped with a wooden tower. It was used as a lookout post at the time of the Spanish Armada. Access to this English Heritage site is denied to the public but it can be viewed from the footpath leading to the harbour.

The battlefield of Hastings, like so many battlefields, is disappointing. Though part of the ground has been preserved and is managed by the English Heritage, the buildings and roads around the site confuse the eye. It is the remains of Battle Abbey(TQ 748157), which sit squarely upon Senlac Hill, that cause the most difficulty. This is where the English shield wall was formed and where Harold fell and died. Telham Hill (TQ 755138), where William first caught sight of the English positions, can be reached by car or on foot. The view from Telham Hill, however, is partially obscured by the walls and trees of the abbey grounds. A road, Powdermill Lane, now runs across the foot of Senlac Hill where the Normans would have formed up to attack. The hedgerows on the north side of the lane and the perimeter of the English Heritage grounds to the east and west, limit the area of the battlefield which can be examined to just the south-facing slopes of Senlac Hill.

An audio tour is included in the admission price to Battle Abbey and the immediate battlefield. There is a book shop inside the courtyard of the Abbey and in the grounds are exhibitions and an introductory video. The point where Harold fell is marked by an inscribed stone. On summer weekends Norman re-enactors parade the grounds. Periodically, there is a re-enactment of the battle on the site, with scores of authentically clad mounted knights and hundreds of Housecarls and Norman infantry providing a spectacular display.

Few of the criticisms of Hastings can be levelled at the battlefield of Lewes. A large part of the battlefield remains open Downland. It is still possible to walk the old route up the northern slope of Offham Hill known as "Simon's track" (TQ 400120) which de Montfort's army took on the morning of 14 May 1264. This is a steep climb up a narrow footpath and can only be taken in single file. The views over Lewes and the Ouse valley are breathtaking and it is easy to see why Henry III placed his only lookout here. The top of the path skirts the disused chalkpit where many burial pits have been discovered.

An alternative route to the battlefield is via Blackcap Hill (TQ 375125) which can be reached along a bridleway from the B2116. It is likely that some men of the baron's army reached the battlefield from Blackcap Hill. A public footpath/bridleway runs across the top of Blackcap Hill and Mount Harry directly onto the battlefield as does Simon's track.

De Montfort's army was drawn up in a position that ran approximately south-west to north-west in line with the present-day horse stables to the upper slopes of Offham Hill. The entire position can be walked, allowing the visitor almost the same view of the battlefield as Simon de Montfort. Though Lewes has grown far beyond its town walls, the keep of the castle can still be seen from Offham Hill. A public byway joins the stables (where the grandstand of the long-abandoned Lewes Racecourse was once located) with the Offham Road (the A275). Approximately half-way down this byway is a public footpath across the fields to the houses of Landport Bottom. By following this footpath the visitor can walk across the lower slopes up which Henry's and Edward's forces advanced, and the gradient of the ascent can be fully appreciated.

By returning to the stables the visitor can follow the bridleway towards H.M. Prison Lewes. This is the route taken by the Royalists, both in their attack and their retreat. Because of the lie of the land Offham Hill is not visible from this track. At some point is the site of "King Harry's Mill" where Richard of Cornwall sought refuge. The circular mound, which comprised the only remains of the windmill, was reported by Professor Sir Maurice Powicke to still be in existence in 1964.

The remains of the Priory of St. Pancras, where Henry set up his headquarters before the battle and to which place he retreated after the battle, are open to the public on Tuesday and Thursday afternoons from April to September. A magnificent memorial to the battle in the shape of a knight's helmet stands in the grounds of the priory (TQ 414095) and is freely accessible to the public at all times. Around the top of the monument are scenes from the time of the battle, including a fine image of Simon de Montford. The memorial is also decorated by lines from the *Song of Lewes*. Next to the Priory is a large mound, some twenty-four feet high. This is the motte of the original castle built at Lewes in the years immediately following the Battle of Hastings.

A reproduction of the "bombard" found in the moat of Bodiam Castle. It is currently on display in one of the towers of the Castle. (By kind permission of the Director of Bodium Castle and the National Trust).

Amberley Castle (TQ 028132), a product of the Hundred Years War, has remained in private ownership and, since 1989, has been an hotel and restaurant of the highest order. The general public can view the castle and grounds but strictly by appointment only. It is still possible to mount part of the forty-feet high walls and inside the castle are suits of armour, bills and pikes, and a crossbow. The restaurant serves excellent food in the most perfect setting Sussex has to offer the military historian!

Bodiam Castle (TQ 785256) is one of the finest late-medieval castles in England. With its mighty towers reflected in the still waters of its vast moat, Bodiam Castle is magnificent. The exterior of the castle is in excellent condition and it is possible to climb the original steep, spiral staircases to reach the top of the gatehouse and one of the drum towers. Little remains of its internal buildings but in the base of one of the towers is a replica of the bombard cannon which was dredged out of the moat. In the gatehouse can be seen an original portcullis and the "murder holes" through which the defenders could drop objects - such as stones or boiling oil - upon the attackers. Within the castle grounds is a small

museum with displays which include stone and iron shot, a Bill hook and a scale model of the castle in its heyday.

Herstmonceux Castle (TQ 646104), though built by a soldier in war time, was of only limited military value. It has rising ground to the north, east and west, its gun ports are virtually useless and the water-filled moat encompasses only three sides of the castle walls. However, the enemies of the day were the French and all that they had been able to achieve during the Hundred Years War were hit-and-run raids. Herstmonceux would have been quite capable of resisting such assaults. The grounds and gardens are open to the public, from which all sides of the castle can be inspected. Guided tours of the castle interior, which houses a working Study Centre, can be undertaken by prior arrangement.

Michelham Priory, near Arlington (TQ 558093), also dates from the Hundred Years War. This fortified monastery has a late-14th century gatehouse with walls sixty feet high and four feet thick. It has a wet ditch and access to the Priory was originally over a wooden drawbridge. The Priory is open from March to October.

Rye's former role in the wars against the French is still recalled at it's castle, the Ypres Tower, which is now a local museum. In front of the Tower is the Gun Garden, complete with cannon. All that remains of Rye's perimeter defences, however, are the imposing Land Gate and a short section of the stone wall built to protect the exposed northern side of the town.

Winchelsea's defences date from just before the outbreak of the Hundred Years War. The remains of it's three gateways - the New Gate, the Pipewell Gate and the impressive Strand Gate - still stand. In front of the New Gate can be seen the start of the huge ditch which protected the whole of the eastern side of the town.

Between Rye and Winchelsea is Henry VIII's Camber Castle, which is open to visitors for just a few weekends in the summer. Though it's outer walls remain largely intact, the internal stonework has been badly damaged (TQ 922185).

At the same time that Henry was building his artillery castle at Camber, the first cannon in England to be cast as a single piece was made by the iron-master Ralph Hogg. His home, appropriately called Hogg House, can be seen by the entrance to Buxted Park on the A272.

Many of the former fire beacon sites used to warn of the approach of the Spanish Armada are on public land and can be reached by footpath. A number of the beacons were located in old Celtic hill forts, such as The Trundle and Highdown Hill. Some of the others can be can be identified by their names, for example Firle Beacon (TQ 485059), Ditchling Beacon (TQ 333132) and Beacon Hill at Bishopstone (TQ 476017). Rottingdean also has a Beacon Hill which is crowned with a monument on the beacon site (TQ 366024).

The walk across the fields from Rye to Camber Castle goes besides, and then across, part of the *Royal Military Canal*, which reaches its conclusion at Cliff End (TQ 894138). It is possible to walk along the towpath for most of the canal's twenty-eight mile length with the Royal Military Canal Path marked with blue and yellow signs. It is hard to believe that during the Napoleonic Wars this lovely little waterway was considered a formidable defensive barrier.

From this era a surprisingly large number of Martello Towers still stand. The most westerly of this chain of forts, No.74 at Seaford, (TV 485985) is now a local museum and is open to the public most weekends. With a cannon mounted on its roof, this fort provides a very good image of how a Martello Tower would have looked in the first decade of the nineteenth century. Further east, No.73, known as the Wish Tower, is situated to the west of the pier along the sea-front at Eastbourne (TV 613983). For a short period of time this was a Napoleonic museum run by the local council. No.66 at Langney Point close to Sovereign Harbour is in reasonable condition, having been taken over by the Coastguard Service as a lookout tower, though it is no longer occupied. To the east of Sovereign Harbour, at the Crumbles, is No.64. This tower is sealed and has not been maintained. No.62 - the Grey Tower - is a private residence located in the Martello

One of a pair of cannon which originally stood at the entrance to a depot built on Horsham Common to house the arms of the troops in Horsham Barracks during the Napoleonic Wars. Currently these are on display at Horsham Museum, (TQ 173304). (By kind permission of the Curator, Horsham Museum).

Beach Park caravan site. Nos. 61 and 60 are also private residences. The former (TQ 653035) is in remarkably good condition. In WWII it was used as an observation post for No.237 Coast Battery. The brickwork of No.55 at the western edge of Norman's Bay (TQ 684053) is deteriorating and the building is unsafe, though planning permission has been granted for its renovation and conversion into a two-bedroom house. No.28, overlooks the estuary of the River Rother at Rye harbour (TQ 942188). It is now in very poor condition. No.30 is situated on the northern side of the A259 Winchelsea to Rye road, almost directly opposite Rye Harbour Road (TQ 918198). It was sited to defend the nearby sluices of the Royal Military Canal. It now sits on waste land close to new housing.

The Eastbourne Circular Redoubt was the largest fortification built in Sussex during the Napoleonic Wars and it is still almost entirely intact (TV 623997). It is possible to walk around the parade ground and climb the walls to inspect a 32-pounder gun, on its traversing platform, which once formed part of the fortress's armament. Within the casemates is the Sussex Combined Services Museum. This first-class exhibition includes a large model of the Redoubt, as it was originally constructed in 1810, and a cut-away model of the other Napoleonic fort in Eastbourne, the Wish Tower. The main display is that of the uniforms, weapons, medals and other memorabilia of the Royal Sussex Regiment. There are also rooms dedicated to the presence in Sussex of the RAF, the Royal Artillery and the Royal Navy, including the Royal Marines. The museum also houses the Museum of the Queen's Royal Irish Hussars, its link with Sussex being that the 4th and 8th Hussars which combined to form this regiment were previously stationed at Lewes and Brighton. At the entrance to the fortress is a Centurion Tank once used by the Royal Irish Hussars in Korea in 1951. Admission to the Redoubt is free but a small charge is made to view the museum.

Behxhill-on-Sea's former importance as a barracks during Napoleonic times is recalled with a display of artefacts in the town's museum. Bexhill was one of the principle barracks of the King's German Legion which was composed mainly of soldiers from King George III's Hanoverian possessions. The items on display include a diorama of part of the battlefield of Waterloo, flags, portraits, and a brief history of this once-famous corps.

The Littlehampton East Bank Battery of 1760 now sits on the edge of the amusement park close to the mouth of the River

× Arun

Adur. Part of its earthen ramparts are visible but they are covered in shrubs and are scarcely recognisable as defensive works. Across the river, the West Bank Fort is no longer accessible to the general public but remains of the ramparts, part of the Carnot wall and one of the open bastions can be viewed from a public boardwalk which cuts through the sand dunes on the edge of West Beach (TQ 028012).

Shoreham Redoubt of 1857, though built in the same decade as the Littlehampton Fort, is in a much better condition. Apart from the removal of the barracks and rear walls, and considerable silting in the ditches, the fort is largely intact. It sits on the western arm of the harbour entrance with an uninterrupted view of the sea (TQ 233045). The fort is freely open to the general public and it is possible to walk around the parade ground and the gun emplacements but not the internal passages or inside the caponniers, the latter being blocked with debris.

Newhaven Fort (TQ 449001) has been completely refurbished after being allowed to fall into ruin following the departure of the Army in 1962. It is now a leading tourist attraction open most of the year, with its barrack rooms displaying a wide range of military exhibits. Amongst the excellent displays are re-creations of an Ops Room at the time of the Battle of Britain and of the Royal Observer Corps in its Cold War nuclear fall-out detection role. Newhaven was the principle departure port for the disastrous raid upon Dieppe in 1942 and the terror and confusion of this abortive mission are brought to life in an impressive audio-visual display.

The ramparts of the fort can be walked in their entirety and the 12-pounder and 6-inch gun emplacements - with each type of gun in situ - can be inspected. The views from the ramparts over the harbour and along the coast are wonderful as is the climb down the tunnel cut through the chalk to the Caponnier at the foot of the cliffs.

Though now overgrown, gun emplacements and magazines of the Lower Battery of 1855 can also be found at the bottom of the cliffs, between the Caponnier and the harbour entrance. On the cliff top beyond the confines of the fort are the well-preserved remains of a 1940s Emergency Coastal Battery.

Almost nothing remains of the Langney Redoubt. Just three iron gun pivots and part of a gun emplacement stand isolated close to the water's edge (TQ 643011) at Langney Point near to Martello Tower No.66.

There are so many reminders of World War II throughout Sussex that entire books have been written on the subject (see Bibliography). Pillboxes, and the remains of gun and searchlight emplacements, still look out from points of tactical importance and a stroll along a quiet Downland path is often a walk over one of the many tank roads that were laid in 1940. The most impressive concentration of pillboxes is at Barcombe Mills where ten works defended the tidal limit of the Ouse and the Newhaven to Lewes railway line. These formed part of the General Headquarters Line.

Most of the coastal defences of the 1940s, which formed what was known as the "coastal crust", have disappeared. However at Cuckmere Haven, one of the few relatively undeveloped areas of the Sussex coast, many of the defences of 1940-2 still remain. To the west of the River Cuckmere estuary is an anti-tank wall and, to the east, an anti-tank ditch and heavy machine gun posts blend into the foot of the Downs. Guarding the beaches at Pett Level was an Emergency Coastal Battery (TQ 891135). The Battery Observation post and the Gun House are still largely intact.

Located close to the remains of the old runway at Tangmere is the Military Aviation Museum. As well as a fine display of medals, models, dioramas, uniforms and photographs the museum boasts a hall which houses a Hurricane and two Spitfires, one of which is an unusual early prototype. The Merston Hall also exhibits aircraft from Tangmere's post-war period. These include two aircraft that broke the world air speed record. The Gloster Meteor which established the record in 1946 and a Hawker Hunter, also flown from Tangmere, which achieved a new record in 1953, can both be seen. Outside the

A 32-pounder muzzle-loading gun on a traversing carriage on the gun platform of the Eastbourne Redoubt. (By kind permission of the Sussex Combined Services Museum, Eastbourne Redoubt).

museum building other aircraft from the post-war period, not all of which have a direct relationship with Tangmere, are on display along with a number of military vehicles. Adjacent to the museum is a section of the runway at the end of which is the old Control Tower. Sadly, this historic building is not maintained and it is now in a poor condition. A few hundred yards down the road from the old airfield is the Bader Arms public house.

Shoreham Airport is home to the Museum of D-Day Aviation. Incorporating within its structure a Blister hangar, this small museum has a number of unusual displays. These are a section of a Horsa Glider, typical of those used in Operation Overlord, a room dedicated to the Air Sea Rescue branch (of which Shoreham airport was a host) and large sections dedicated to the Hawker Typhoon. At the rear of the museum is a full-scale replica of a Spitfire in D-Day markings. The museum is open from April to October and at weekends in March and November.

Shoreham also hosts an annual Royal Air Force Association Battle of Britain Airshow at the beginning of September. This excellent event, which usually includes the Hurricane, Spitfire and Lancaster of the Battle of Britain Memorial flight and the incomparable Harrier amongst its many flying displays, also has static exhibits of aircraft from every period of military aviation history.

Ford airfield, the former Fleet Air Arm base, is now the site of a weekly Sunday market which is held on part of the old runway. However, a Hawker Hunter in Naval markings sits proudly above the market entrance to remind us all of its military past which began in WWI and continued until 1958.

RAF Deanland (TQ 516114) was re-born in the 1990s as a small private airfield from which light aircraft, including microlights, still fly. Westhampnett, now known as Goodwood Aerodrome, also flourishes as a private airfield with many of the original buildings still standing around the site.

Areas of the Ashdown Forest are still designated for military use and are not readily accessible to the public. However, the remains of an Army camp can be seen to the west of Chucks Hatch (TQ 465 333) and the public can walk the length of the WWII Emergency Landing Ground near Wych Cross (TQ 426305). The former Cold War radio installation can be seen from Camp Hill though the site is in a restricted area controlled and used by Sussex Police.

Thorney Island is the last military establishment on the Sussex coast still in the hands of the Ministry of Defence. Now known as Baker Barracks, it is the home of the 47th (Hampshire and Sussex) Regiment of Royal Artillery. Access to the barracks is strictly controlled by the Army, but a public footpath runs around the entire island. All walkers have to give their names and addresses before being allowed to follow the footpath through MOD property. The airfield can clearly be seen from the footpath and one of the runways is still used.

A military presence is also maintained at the Roussillon Barracks just north of Chichester on the A286 towards Midhurst. From 1873 until 1960 the barracks had been the Regimental Depot of the Royal Sussex Regiment. In 1964 it became a Training School of the Royal Military Police. The barracks are named after the French Roussillion Regiment which was defeated by the Sussex Regiment at the Battle of Quebec in 1759.

In The Keep of the barracks is housed the Royal Military Police Museum. It is open on weekdays throughout the year and weekends during the Summer. Admission is free, although visitors must report to the Guardhouse and sign a visitors' log before entry is granted. This compact museum depicts in paintings, photographs and words the surprisingly varied roles that have been performed by the R.M.P. and the provosts since 1511. There are fine examples of uniforms, including those of the Mounted Troop and the Airborne Company, some of which are for sale in the small museum shop.

This then is the physical evidence of Sussex's military past. The true legacy of centuries of armed struggle against oppressive monarchs and aggressive invaders, however, is the freedom and democracy we now enjoy. In pursuit of these ideals the shores, seas and skies of Sussex have been the scenes of terrible slaughter. It should never be forgotten that the peace and prosperity we take for granted was won by the sword and defended by the gun.

A Centurion tank of the Queen's Royal Irish Hussars, situated in the grounds of the Eastbourne Redoubt.

NOTES

Celts and Centurions

1. D. Harrison, *Along the South Downs*, p.3. R. Bradley "Stock Raising and the Origin of the Hill Forts on the South Downs. *The Antiquaries' Journal*, Vol. 51 (1971), pp.8-29.
2. J. Armstrong, *A History of Sussex*, p.24. R. Penn, *Portrait of Ashdown Forest*, p.109. Other Iron Age forts in Sussex are to be found at Harting Down, Harrow Hill, Thundersbarrow, Offham Hill, Seaford Head, Saxonbury and Philpots in the High Weald and Castle Hill at Newhaven, see K. Leslie & B. Short, *An Historical Atlas of Sussex*, pp.20-3.
3. At Maiden Castle as many as 22,260 stones were found in a pit at one of the gateways; J. Dyer, *Ancient Britain*, p.126.
4. Harrison, p.9.
5. B. Darby, *The South Downs*, pp.82-3.
6. P. Beresford Ellis, *Caesar's Invasion of Britain*, p.70.
7. T. Newark, *Celtic Warriors*, p.18.
8. A. Down, *Roman Chichester*, pp.3-5, 7 & 52-4. Armstrong, *A History of Sussex*, p.25. G. Blaxland, *South-East Britain, Eternal Battleground*, p.28.
9. The other Saxon Shore forts were at Reculver, Richborough, Dover, Lympne and Porchester. E. Tetlow, *The Enigma of Hastings*, p.133.
10. Down, p.18.
11. Blaxland, p.35.

South Saxons

1. M. Holmes, *King Arthur - A Military History*, pp.70-1.
2. A. Savage, *The Anglo Saxon Chronicles*, p. 29
3. H. Cheal, *The Story of Shoreham*, p.7
4. Savage, p.35.
5. R. Whitlock, *The Warrior Kings of Saxon England*, p.17.
6. Heorepeburan, or Eorpeburan, has also been placed on the eastern Rother a few miles from Northiam, see *An Historical Atlas of Sussex*, pp. 50-1.
7. P. Brandon, *The South Saxons*, pp.182, 183, 185-6.
8. Savage, p.106.
9. D. Seaward, *Sussex*, p.35.
10. Savage, pp.107, 147 & 150-1.
11. J. Grimson, *The Channel Coasts of England*, p.53.

12. R. Abels, "Bookland and Fyrd Service in Late Saxon England", *The Battle of Hastings, Sources & Interpretations*, pp.60 & 68.
13. D. Harries, *Maritime Sussex*, p.9.
14. Here is one of History's greatest ironies. The Vikings had been using Normandy as a base for their attacks upon the south coast and in 1002 Ethelred married Emma, the sister of Robert Duke of Normandy (William the Conqueror's father), hoping that Richard would then put a stop to such activities. The result of this union was not the end of the raids but the invasion of England by the Normans in 1066!

Conquerors and Castles

1. Tetlow, *The Enigma of Hastings*. pp.62-4.
2. R. Wace, *Le Roman de Rou*, quoted by A. Clarke in *A day that made History*, p.6. A hauberk was a chain-mail tunic.
3. J. Gillingham, "William the Bastard at War", *The Battle of Hastings. Sources & Interpretations*, p.102.
4. Ibid, p.112.
5. Ibid, p.107.
6. S. Morillo, *The Battle of Hastings. Sources & Interpretations*, xxiv. E. Tetlow, pp.152-6. Strangely, we have no archaeological evidence for the exact site of the battle as there is no record of any bones or metal ever having been found on Battle Hill.
7. D. Howarth, 1066, p.170.
8. M. Chibnall, "Military Service in Normandy before 1066", in *The Battle of Hastings, Sources & Interpretations*, p.90.
9. G. Regan, *Famous British Battles*, p.6.
10. S. Morillo, p.152.
11. M. Phillips, 1066 - *Origin of a Nation*, p.19.
12. A. Clarke, *A day that made History*, p.20.
13. Ibid.
14. C. Lemmon, *The Field of Hastings*, p.44. D. Butler, *1066 The Story of a Year*, p.246.
15. B. Bachrach, "The Feigned Retreat at Hastings", in *The Battle of Hastings, Sources & Interpretations*, p.190.
16. Clarke, ibid, p25.
17. Ibid, p.26.
18. M. Rud, *The Bayeux Tapestry*, p.89.

19. Clarke, p.52.
20. J. Guy, *Castles in Sussex*, p.128.

Democracy's Dawn
1. C. Lee, *This Sceptred Isle*, p.88.
2. M. Powicke, *The Battle of Lewes 1264*, pp. 22-3.
3. B. Fleming, *1264 The Battle of Lewes*, p.16.
4. D. Carpenter, *The Battles of Lewes & Evesham*, p.21.
5. Ibid
6. Powicke, p.109.
7. Ibid, p.110.
8. Carpenter, p.25.
9. J. P. Gilson, "An unpublished notice of the battle of Lewes", *English Historical Review, xi* (1896), pp. 520-22.
10. Carpenter, p.26.
11. Ibid, p.32.
12. In 1257 Richard was elected to succeed William of Holland as Holy Roman Emperor. He was never officially crowned and he usually adopted the marginally less presumptuous title of "King of the Romans."
13. Powicke, p.118.
14. G. Blaxland, *South-East Britain, Eternal Battleground*, p.77.
15. There were at least three fords, one at Southerham, one by Old Malling Farm and another by the bridge. T. Beamish, *Battle Royal*, pp.155-6.
16. Ibid, p.78.
17. M. Wade Labarge, *Simon de Montfort*, p.230.

Defence of the Realm
1. J. Foster, *The Rye Guide*, pp.46-7.
2. I. Green, *The Book of the Cinque Ports*, p.17
3. J. Collard, *Maritime Rye*, pp12-3.
4. M. Bentall, *The Cinque Ports*, pp.121 & 145-7.
5. Ibid, p.163.
6. D. Seaward, *Sussex*, pp.12 & 179.
7. J. Guy, *Catles in Sussex*, p.32.
8. Ibid, p.34.
9. A. Bryant, *Freedom's Own Island*, p.122.
10. J. Goring, *Sussex and the Spanish Armada*, p.5.
11. A. Ankers, *Sussex Cavalcade*, p.129.
12. J. Goring, *Ibid*, pp.5-6.
13. J. Goodwin, *The Military Defence of West Sussex*, pp.13-16. L. Boynton, *The Elizabethan Militia*, pp.159-63.

14. Goodwin, *Ibid*, pp.11-12.
15. Boynton, *ibid*, p.132.
16. Green, *ibid*, p.29. J. Collard, p.24.
17. P Kemp, *The Campaign of the Spanish Armada*, p.135.
18. J. Parry, *The Coast of Sussex*, pp.212-4.

King against Country
1. P. Brandon & B. Short, *The South East from AD 1000*, p.147.
2. G. Blaxland, *South-East Britain, Eternal Battleground*, p.94
3. J. Guy, *Castles in Sussex*, p.24.
4. C. Thomas-Standford, *Sussex in the Great Civil War*, p.9.
5. A. Ankers, *Sussex Cavalcade*, pp.45-6 & 129.
6. P. Haythornewaite, *The English Civil War*, pp.24-56.
7. A. Fletcher, *Sussex 1600-1660*, pp.267-8.
8. Thomas-Standford, *ibid*, p.16.
9. Fletcher, *ibid*, p.272. Rowkeshill, or Rooks Hill, was the name for The Trundle at that time because a medieval chapel dedicated to St. Roche still stood on its summit, J. Armstrong, *A History of Sussex*, p..98.
10. Armstrong, *ibid*, p.95.
11. D. Seaward, *Sussex*, p.151.

Bastion Shore
1. M. Brentnall, *The Cinque Ports*, 163.
2. C. Barnett, *Britain and her Army*, pp.187-90.
3. J. Parry, *The Coast of Sussex*, p.27. J. Goodwin, *Fortification of the South Coast*, p.2.
4. R. Grant, *The Brighton Garrison*, pp.12-15.
5. K. Leslie, *An Historical Atlas of Sussex*, pp.51-2. R. Cusick, "Signalling systems in use during the wars with France". *The Waterloo Journal*, December 2000, pp.5-14.
6. *Fortification of the South Coast*, p.16.
7. C. Woodford, *By the Crown Divided*, p.15.
8. S. Sutcliff, *Martello Towers*, p.47
9. G. Hutchinson, *The Royal Military Canal*, pp.9-11.
10. The precise dimensions of the towers varied slightly from builder to builder, see S. Sutcliffe, *Martello Towers*, pp.64-79. The figures here are those given by J. Goodwin, *Fortification of the South Coast*, pp.10-11.
11. J. Goodwin, *The Military Defence of West Sussex*, pp.28-42.
12. *ibid*, pp.45-51.

The World at War

1. J. Goodwin, *The Military Defence of West Sussex*, p.75.
2. P. Longstaff-Tyrrell, *Tyrrell's List*, pp.10 & 19. B. Willard, *The Forest*, p.65.
3. R. Brooks, *Sussex Flights and Fliers*, p.117-20.
4. M . Taylor, *This was Rustington, In Times of War*, pp.2-9.
5. D. Harries, *Maritime Sussex*, pp.105-6.
6. K. Leslie, *An Historical Atlas of Sussex*, pp.58-9.
7. C. Alexander, *Ironside's Line*, pp.11-14.
8. G. Ellis, *The Secret Tunnels of South Heighton*, pp.51-4.
9. P. Longstaff-Tyrrell, *Operation Cuckmere Haven*, p. 18. *Tyrrell's List*, p.7.
10. G. Hutchinson, *The Royal Military Canal*, p.16.
11. M. Mace, *Sussex Wartime Relics and Memorials*, pp.21-2.
12. Alexander, pp.64-5 & 74.
13. Sussex Express and County Herald, *The War in East Sussex*, p.17.
14. M. Mace, *Frontline Sussex*, p.15.
15. D. Rowland, *Coastal Blitz*, pp.75-79.
16. *Tyrrell's List*, pp.11 & 19; M. Mace, *Relics and Memorials*, pp.49-50.

Savage Skies

1. D. Wood, *Target England*, pp.7-9.
   Actual numbers vary from one source to another, see N. Franks, *Fighter Command*, p.71; A. Ward, *A Nation Alone*, p.94; L. Deighton, *Battle of Britain*, p.101; R.Brooks, *Sussex Airfields in the Second World War*, p.12.
2. Ward, *ibid*, pp.86-9.
3. A. Saunders, *Channel Defences*, p.101.
4. Deighton, pp.97-101.
5. *Ibid*, pp.100-1.
6. E. Bishop, *Their Finest Hour*, p.40.
7. D. Rowland, *Spitfires over Sussex*, pp.37 & 40.
8. Burgess & Saunders, *Battle over Sussex*, 1940, pp.55-9.
9. Brooks, *Sussex Airfields*, pp.48-50.
10. *Ibid*, pp.68-70.
11. Wood, *ibid* p.124.
12. Ward, *ibid*, pp.154-8.
13. *Battle over Sussex*, pp.93-5.

Dieppe to D-Day

1. D. Sarkar, *Bader's Tangmere Spitfires*, p.28.
2. Burgess & Saunders, *Blitz over Sussex*, p.75.
3. R. Brooks, *Sussex Airfields*, pp.160-2.
4. *Ibid*, pp.149-53.
5. *Ibid*, pp.163-4.
6. *Ibid*, pp.153-5.
7. P. Longstaff-Tyrrell, *Operation Cuckmere Haven*, pp.45-6.
8. D. & S. Whitaker, *Dieppe*, p.227.
9. J. Gardiner, *D-Day, Those who were there*, p.33.
10. I. Greig, *D-Day West Sussex*, pp.12-4.
11. *Ibid*, pp.10-11.
12. *Tyrrell's List*, p.23.
13. Grieg, *ibid*, pp.46-52. One of the Mulberry units sank off Pagham harbour and is now a popular diving site, see M. Mace, *Relics & Memorials*, p.142.
14. Grieg, pp.89-90.
15. K. Delve, *D-Day The Air Battle*, pp. 136-8.
16. P. Burgess & A. Saunders, *Bombers over Sussex 1943-45*.

The Sussex Soldier

1. L. Boynton, *The Elizabethan Militia*, p.9.
2. C. Barnett, *Britain and her Army*, pp.112, 172 & 282.
3. R. Glover, *Britain at Bay*, pp.211-17.
4. R. Cusick, *Barrack's, Bounties and Beer in Sharpe's Horsham*, paper presented to Horsham Museum Society. (April 2000).
5. J. Odam, *The Seaford Story*, pp.28-31.
6. The regiments were: The East Norfolks, The Berkshires, The West Essex, The Oxfords, The North Devons, The Westminster/Middlesex, The West Suffolks, The South Devons, The North Hants, The Dorsets, and the East Middlesex. R. Grant, *The Brighton Garrison*, pp.12-13.
7. R. Grant, *ibid*, p.76.
8. P. Crook, *The Sussex Home Guard*, p.11.
9. Crook, *ibid*, pp. 4, 26-7 & 73-8.
10. S. Angell, *The Secret Sussex Resistance*, p.59.
11. J. Ainsworth, *The Royal Sussex Regiment*, pp.3-13.
12. J. Haswell, *The Queen's Regiment*, pp.20-1.
13. B. Peedle, *The Modern Territorial Army*, p.9.

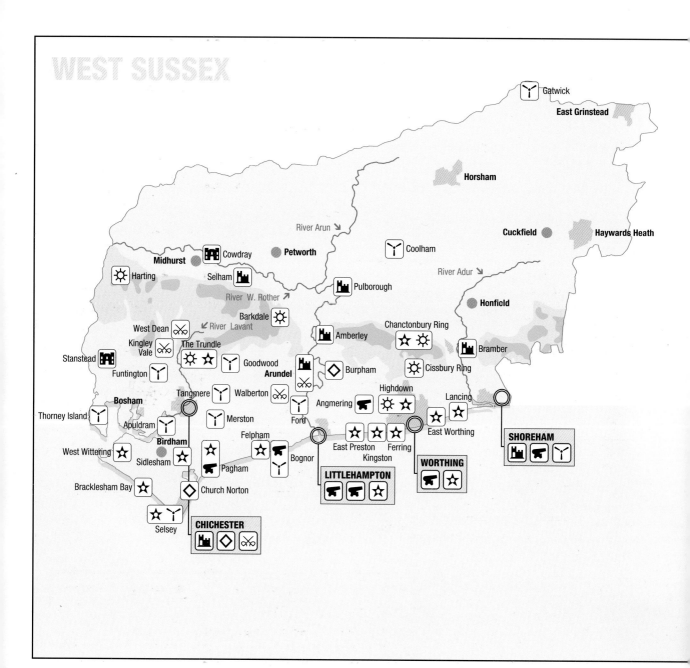

WEST SUSSEX

Gatwick

East Grinstead

Horsham

River Arun

Cuckfield

Haywards Heath

Coolham

Petworth

Midhurst   Cowdray

River Adur

Harting   Selham

River W. Rother

Pulborough   Honfield

Barkdale

West Dean   River Lavant

Amberley   Chanctonbury Ring

Kingley Vale   The Trundle

Bramber

Stanstead   Goodwood   Burpham   Cissbury Ring

Funtington   Arundel

Thorney Island   Tangmere   Walberton   Highdown   Lancing

Bosham   Angmering   East Worthing

Apuldram   Merston   Ford

West Wittering   Birdham   Felpham   East Preston   Ferring

Sidlesham   Pagham   Bognor   Kingston   SHOREHAM

Bracklesham Bay   Church Norton   LITTLEHAMPTON   WORTHING

Selsey   CHICHESTER

EAST SUSSEX

Hammerwood
High Rocks
Scotney
Hartfield
Crowborough
Hawkhurst
River Rother
Royal Military Canal
Bodium
Northiam
Burwash
River Ouse
RYE
28
Cross-in-Hand
Heathfield
Uckfield
Camber
Chailey
Winchelsea
LEWES
Isfield
River Cuckmere
Battle
Ditchling
Fulking
Ranscombe
Fairlight
Devils Dyke
Lewes
Deanland
Herstmonceux
Hailsham
HASTINGS
Hollingbury
Mt. Caburn
Cooden Down
Bexhill
Michelham
Whitehawk
Firle
Coombe Hill
Normans Bay
55
Aldrington
Bishopstone
Wilmington
PEVENSEY
Rottingdean
Langley
66
BRIGHTON
Polegate
Friston
EASTBOURNE
NEWHAVEN
SEAFORD
Belle Tout
73
74
Beachy Head
Beachy Head

	CASTLE		HILL FORT		MARTELLO'S (WITH NUMBER)
	FORTIFIED HOUSE		BATTLE		BEACON
	FORTIFIED LOCALITY		FORTS AND BATTERIES		AIRFIELD

BIBLIOGRAPHY

Ainsworth, J.	The Royal Sussex Regiment.	(Derby, 1972).
Alcock, L	Arthur's Britain. History and Archaeology AD 367-634.	(Harmondsworth 1971).
Alexander, C.	Ironside's Line, The definitive guide to the General Headquarters Line planned for Great Britain in response to the threat of German invasion 1940-42.	(Storrington 1999).
Angell, S.	The Secret Sussex Resistance	(Midhurst 1996).
Ankers, A.	Sussex Cavalcade.	(Sevenoaks 1992).
Armstrong, J.R.	A History of Sussex.	(Chichester 1961).
Barnett, C.	Britain and her Army 1509-1970.	(London 1970).
Beamish, T.	Battle Royal. The Battle of Lewes.	(London 1978).
Bishop, E.	Their Finest Hour, the story of the Battle of Britain.	(London 1972).
Blaxland,	G. South-East Britain: Eternal Battleground.	(Rainham 1981).
Boynton, L.	The Elizabeathan Militia 1558-1638.	(London 1967).
Brandon, P.	The Sussex Landscape.	(London 1974).
	The South Saxons.	(Chichester 1978).
Brandon, P. & Short, B.	The South East from AD 1000,	(Harlow 1990).
Bradbury, J.	The Battle of Hastings.	(Stroud 1998).
Bradley, R.	"Stock Raising and the Origin of the Hill Forts on the South Downs".	The Antuquaries' Journal, Vol.51 (1971).
Bryant, A.	Freedom's Own Island.	(London 1986).
Brooks, R.	Sussex Airfields in the Second World War.	(Newbury 1993).
	Sussex Flights and Fliers 1783-1919.	(Shoreham-by-Sea 1992).
Bugler, W.	The Story of a Sussex Gunner Regiment.	(Privately published 1982).
Burk, J.	Sussex.	(London 1974).
Butler, D.	1066 The Story of a Year.	(London 1965).
Burgess, P/Saunders, A.	Battle over Sussex 1940.	(Midhurst 1990).
	Blitz over Sussex 1941-42.	(Midhurst 1994).
	Bombers over Sussex 1943-45.	(Midhurst 1995).
Carpenter, D.	The Battles of Lewes & Evesham 1264/5.	(Keele 1987).
Cheal, H.	The Story of Shoreham.	(Hove 1921).
Clark, D.	Battlefield Walks: The South.	(Stroud 1996).
Clarke, A.	The Battle of Hastings: a day that made history.	(London 1988).
Collard, J.	Maritime Rye	(Rye 1978).
Collier, R.	D-Day.	(London 1992).
Corum, M.	D-Day: Brighton Remembers.	(Brighton 1994).
Crook, P	Sussex Home Guard	(Midhurst 1998)
Cusick, R.	"Signalling systems in use during the wars with France".	The Waterloo Journal, December 2000.
Darby, B.	A View of Sussex.	(London 1975).
Darby, B.	The South Downs.	(London 1976).

Deighton, L.	*Battle of Britain.*	(London 1980).
Delve, K.	*D-Day, The Air Battle.*	(London 1994).
Denny, N.		
& Filmer-Sankey, J.	*The Bayeux Tapestry.*	(London 1966).
Down, A,	*Roman Chichester,*	(Chichester 1988).
Ellis, Beresford E.	*Caesar's Invasion of Britain.*	(London, 1978).
Ellis, G.	*The Secret Tunnels of South Heighton,*	(Seaford 1996).
Fleming, B.	*1264 The Battle of Lewes.*	(Hailsham, 1999).
Fletcher, A.	*Sussex 1600-1660, A County Community in Peace and War.*	(Chichester 1980).
J. Foster & K. Clark,	*The Rye Guide.*	(Rye 1997).
Franks, N.	*RAF Fighter Command, 1936-1968.*	(Sparkford 1992).
Gardiner, J.	*D-Day, Those Who Were There.*	(London 1994).
Glover, R.	*Britain at Bay. Defence against Bonaparte, 1803-14.*	(London 1973).
Goodwin, J.	*Fortifications of the South Coast. The Pevensey, Eastbourne and Newhaven Defences 1750-1945.*	(Goring-by-sea 1994)
	The Military Defence of West Sussex. 500 years of fortification of the coast between Brighton and Selsey.	(Midhurst 1985).
Goring, J.	*Sussex and the Spanish Armada.*	(Lewes 1988).
Grant. R.C.	*The Brighton Garrison 1793-1900.*	(Worthing 1997).
Green, I.	*The Book of the Cinque Ports.*	(Buckingham 1984).
Greig, I.	*D-Day West Sussex: Springboard for the Normandy Landings 1944.*	(Chichester 1994).
Grimson, J.	*The Channel Coasts of England.*	(London 1978).
Guy, J.	*Castles in Sussex.*	(Chichester 1984).
Haes, E.	*Natural History of Sussex.*	(Hassocks, 1977).
Harries, D.	*Maritime Sussex.*	(Seaford 1997).
Haswell, J.	*The Queen's Regiment.*	(Canterbury 1985).
Haythornwaite, P.	*The English Civil War 1642-1651. An Illustrated Military History.*	(London 1983).
Harrison, D.	*Along the South Downs.*	(London 1975).
Hillier, D.	*The Bulwark Shore.*	(London 1980).
Hogg, I.	*Hill Forts of Britain.*	(London 1975).
Holmes, M.	*King Arthur - A Military History.*	(London 1998).
Hutchinson, G.	*The Royal Military Canal.*	(Hastings 1995).
Howarth, D.	*1066 The Year of the Conquest.*	(London 1977).
Kemp, P.	*The Campaign of the Spanish Armada.*	(Oxford 1988).
Kenyon, J..R.	*"A Hitherto Unknown Early Seventeenth Century Survey of the Coastal Forts of Southern England".*	FORT magazine, Vol. II, 1983.
Kinross, J.	*The Battlefields of Britain.*	(Newton Abbot 1979).
Labarge, M. Wade	*Simon de Montfort.*	(Bath 1972).
Lemmon, C.	*The Field of Hastings.*	(St. Leonards-on-Sea, 1956).
Leslie, K & Short, B.	*An Historical Atlas of Sussex.*	(Chichester 1999).
Longmate, N.	*Defending the Island - Caesar to the Armada.*	(London 1989).
	Island Fortress: The Defence of Great Britain 1603-1945.	(London 1991).
Longstaff-Tyrrell, P.	*Operation Cuckmere Haven,*	(Polegate 1997).

Longstaff-Tyrrell, P.	*Tyrrell's List. The Artefacts of Two Great Wars in Sussex.*	(Polegate 1998).
Mace, M.	*Frontline Sussex. The Defence Lines of West Sussex 1939-45.*	(Storrington 1996).
	Sussex Wartime Relics and Memorials.	(Storrington 1997).
Mackenzie, S.P.	*The Home Guard.*	(Oxford 1996).
Mattingly, G.	*The Defeat of the Spanish Armada.*	(1962).
Maynell,	*Sussex.*	(London 1947).
Mee, A.	*The King's England, Sussex.*	(London 1964).
Morillo, S.	*The Battle of Hastings, Sources & Interpretations.*	(Suffolk 1996).
Morling, L.	*Sussex Sappers. A History of the Sussex Volunteer and Territorial Army Royal Engineer Units from 1890 to 1967.*	
Newark, T.	*War in Britain.*	(London 2000).
Odam, J.	*The Seaford Story.*	(Seaford 1998).
Parry, J.	*An Historical and Descriptive Account of the Coast of Sussex.*	(London 1833).
Peedle, B.	*Encyclopaedia of the Modern Territorial Army.*	(Wellingborough 1990).
Penn, R.	*Portrait of Ashdown Forest.*	(London 1984).
Poole, H.	*Lewes Priory. The Site and its History.*	(Lewes 2000).
Powell-Edwards, H.	*The Sussex Yeomanry & 16th Battalion Royal Sussex Regiment, 1914-18.*	(London1921).
Powicke, M.	*The Battle of Lewes 1264.*	(Lewes 1964).
Rose, C. & Astell, J.	*The Martello Tower at Seaford.*	(Seaford 1970).
Rowland, D.	*Spitfires over Sussex.*	(Peacehaven 2000).
	Coastal Blitz.	(Seaford 2001).
Salter, M.	*The Castles of Sussex.*	(Malvern 2000).
Sarkar, D.	*Bader's Tangmere Spitfires.*	(Sparford 1996).
Saunders, A.	*Channel Defences.*	(London 1997).
Savage, A.	*The Anglo-Saxon Chronicles.*	(London 1982).
Stephen, J.	*The Roman Forts of the Saxon Shore.*	(London 1978).
Seward, D.	*Sussex.*	(London 1995).
Sussex Express and County Herald, *The War in East Sussex.*		(1945).
Sutcliffe, S.	*Martello Towers.*	(Newton Abbot 1972).
Taylor, M,	*This was Rustington, No.3 In Times of War.*	(Rustington 1989).
Terraine, J.	*The Right of the Line, The Royal Air Force in the European War 1939- 1945.*	(Sevenoaks 1988).
Tetlow, E.	*The Enigma of Hastings,*	(London 1974).
Trimen, R.	*An Historical Memoir of the 35th Royal Sussex Regiment of Foot.*	(Southampton 1873).
Newark, T.	*Celtic Warriors 400 BC - AD 1600.*	(Poole 1986).
Ward, A.	*A Nation Alone. The Battle of Britain - 1940.*	(London 1989).
Willard, B.	*Sussex.*	(London 1965).
	The Forest - Ashdown in East Sussex.	(Marsh Barton 1989).
Whitaker, D. and S.	*Dieppe.*	(London 1992).
Whitehead, W.	*Dieppe 1942.*	(Glasgow 1982).
Wood, D.	*Target England,The illustrated history of the Battle of Britain.*	(London 1980).
Woodford, C.	*By the Crown Divided. Hanoverian Sussex 1770-1800.*	(Willingdon 1983).
Yarrow, A.	*The Fortifications of the East Coast. A guide to castles and other defences.*	(Lewes 1979).
Young, P. & Adair, J.	*Hastings to Culloden.*	(London 1964).

INDEX